DISCIPLING

The iCare Revolutionary Sunday School and Bible Study Method

I'm thankful for my friend, Darryl Wilson, and his passion for better preparation and presentation for more effective Bible study.

Ed Stetzer
Billy Graham Distinguished Chair, Wheaton College
Author, *Planting Missional Churches, Lost and Found, Comeback Churches*, and more

I really like this book! It is timely, practical, and thorough. I am delighted to see a new book on Sunday School when many churches have abandoned Sunday School as a "relic" of the past. They have failed to find an effective replacement, and the result has been a decline in small group attendance and a decline in reaching the lost. This book by Darryl focuses on the teacher and the teaching process – the two encounters. If you are a teacher or prospective teacher, you need this book. If you are a pastor, educator, or Sunday School superintendent, you need to get one of these for every teacher and read and discuss it together.

Ken Hemphill
Founding Director of the Center for Church Planting and Revitalization
North Greenville University
Author, *Revitalizing the Sunday Morning Dinosaur* and more

I love the fact that Darryl Wilson begins with the Great Commission as the foundation and builds a case for the necessity of Sunday School. Just as the church must fulfill the Great Commission given to us by Jesus, so the church must give priority to the Sunday School to fulfill the Lord's expectation. May God use this book to accomplish His purpose.

Elmer Towns
Co-Founder, Liberty University
Author, *Fasting for Spiritual Breakthrough* and more

Bible study teachers have a small window of time during each group gathering to nudge their people down the pathway to discipleship. In these times individuals should so encounter God through His Word that they are transformed. This is a most daunting task, but help has arrived! My friend, Darryl Wilson, will first guide you through your individual encounter with God and then your Bible study group's opportunity to encounter God. This is an absolute must read if you are serious about seeing lives conformed to the image of Christ!

Allan Taylor
Director, Church Education Ministry, Lifeway Christian Resources
Author, *Sunday School Matters* and more

It's about time! That's what those who have followed Darryl Wilson's outstanding blog, *Sunday School Revolutionary*, will say about *Discipling*. Great ideas for Sunday School teachers – just like the blog – but in order! Dr. Wilson has missed nothing. This book is a clear, comprehensive, and complete treatment of everything a fully equipped adult teacher needs to know and do. The book's unique contribution is its compelling emphasis on the first encounter as the essential prerequisite for the second encounter. Other books make a similar exhortation, but I know of no other that provides such a helpful "how to." If you are an adult Sunday School teacher, get this book! If you are a leader of adult teachers, get them this book! Read it together. Discuss it. Do it. But be careful; you may become a "Sunday School Revolutionary" too!

David Francis
Director of Sunday School, Lifeway Christian Resources
– Groups Ministry
Author, *One Hundred: Charting a Course Past One Hundred in Sunday School* and more

We desperately need an army of revolutionary teachers. Teachers who don't just cover the material, but change lives. Teachers who love the Word, love their God, and love their people. This book will show you how to be such a teacher.

Josh Hunt
Author, *Good Questions Have Groups Talking*
Coauthor, *Extreme Sunday School Challenge: Engaging Our World Through New Groups*

Do you desire for the Bible study leaders in your church to be ordinary or exceptional? Exceptional leaders fuel the personal growth of the members as well as potential growth in the number of participants in your groups. Darryl Wilson's new book, *Discipling,* is a blueprint for equipping your leaders to be exceptional Bible study teachers. Get this book into their hands and watch as they propel forward in their leadership, ability to teach, and influence over the members of your congregation. It is well written, practical, and a tool that will impact church leaders for years to come!

Steve Parr
Vice President of Staff Coordination and Development,
Georgia Baptist Convention
Author of *Why They Stay, Sunday School That Really WORKS*, and more

Darryl has done much more than just revisit principles and practices that have been rehashed again and again. He's given every teacher a guidebook for creating a biblically functioning Bible study group, a group that will make disciples that make disciples.

Rick Howerton
Regional Consultant, Kentucky Baptist Convention
Author, *A Different Kind of Tribe: Embracing the New Small Group Dynamic* and more

With a driving passion for Sunday School, Darryl Wilson has leveraged his years of experience as a leader and consultant to provide a most practical manual for Sunday School/Small Group teachers. Embracing the guidance given throughout the book will help teachers be more effective. Every Sunday School leader I know desires to be their best. This book can help them do exactly that!

Bruce Raley
Executive Pastor, First Baptist Church Hendersonville, TN

From years of training Bible study teachers to effectively teach God's Word, Darryl Wilson skillfully provides hundreds of practical tips for helping Bible study leaders excel at teaching people the Word of God. Every Bible study teacher should read *Discipling* and keep it as a handy reference. Church leaders would do well to provide a copy of the book for every new Bible teacher or use it as the basis for their teacher training strategy. Teaching for spiritual transformation requires two encounters. The first encounter is the teacher learning from God Himself, the Master Teacher. The second encounter happens in the life of the learner when the teacher prepares and engages learners in exciting Bible studies. This is my new go-to book for training Bible study leaders.

Daryl Eldridge
President, Rockbridge Seminary
Author of *The Teaching Ministry of the Church*

Introductory Video – Enter password "wilson" if prompted.

DISCIPLING

REVOLUTIONARY SUNDAY SCHOOL

DARRYL WILSON

ANEKO
PRESS

Visit Dr. Wilson's website:
www.sundayschoolrevolutionary.com

Discipling – Dr. Darryl H. Wilson
Copyright © 2014, 2017, 2024
Original published in 2017 as *Disciple-Making Encounters*

Cover Design: J. Martin
Editor: S. Wilkinson

Aneko Press

www.anekopress.com

Aneko Press, Life Sentence Publishing, and our logos are trademarks of
Life Sentence Publishing, Inc.
203 E. Birch Street
P.O. Box 652
Abbotsford, WI 54405

RELIGION / Christian Ministry / General
Paperback ISBN: 979-8-88936-280-7
eBook ISBN: 979-8-88936-281-4

10 9 8 7 6 5 6 7 8 9 10

Available where books are sold

CONTENTS

I dedicate this book to Yvonne, my wife and best friend, for believing in me.

I also acknowledge and appreciate the men and women who opened God's Word to me in Bible study groups over the years.

But praise goes to God who called me to Himself through the love and sacrifice of Jesus Christ. May Your disciples fill every nation.

INTRODUCTION

Go, therefore, and make disciples of all nations,
baptizing them in the name of the Father and of the
Son and of the Holy Spirit, teaching them to observe
everything I have commanded you. And remem-
ber, I am with you always, to the end of the age.
(Matt. 28:19-20)

In the Great Commission, Jesus sent His followers to make
disciples of all nations. He told us how: baptize them and
teach them to observe everything He commanded. In pursuit
of obedience, early disciples experienced amazing results in
carrying out their mission of discipling:

And they devoted themselves to the apostles' teach-
ing, to the fellowship, to the breaking of bread, and
to the prayers. Then fear came over everyone, and
many wonders and signs were being performed
through the apostles. Now all the believers were
together and held all things in common. They sold
their possessions and property and distributed the
proceeds to all, as anyone had a need. Every day

they devoted themselves to meeting together in the temple complex, and broke bread from house to house. They ate their food with a joyful and humble attitude, praising God and having favor with all the people. And every day the Lord added to them those who were being saved. (Acts 2:42-47)

Reading about God's work among and through the early believers reminds me of the potential for Sunday School and small groups. When we devote ourselves to God, we:

- understand and live out God's Word;

- eat, fellowship, and care in community;

- pray, worship, and praise; and

- find favor with and salvation for those around us.

In the past two centuries, Bible study groups have helped the church carry out this work. When I refer to Bible study groups, I include both small groups and Sunday School classes (whether at home, church, or another location). Through the context of a small group of people studying God's Word together, lost people have been prayed for, invited in, and cared for. They have been taught, and many have found Jesus. Pastors tell me that 50-100% of the lost who attend their Bible study groups for twelve months accept Jesus as Savior and Lord.

At the same time, the saved have been encouraged, taught, discipled, connected, trained, and mobilized for the harvest. Dr. Thom Rainer, president of Lifeway Christian Resources, discovered that 83% of new church members who become active in Bible study groups and worship services will still be involved in the church five years later, while only 16% of those who only attend worship services will still be involved five years later.[1]

---

1   Steve R. Parr, "Sunday School That Really Works," *Christian Bible Studies*, *www.christianitytoday.com/biblestudies/articles/churchhomeleadership/sunday-school-that-really-works.html* (January 16, 2017).

In too many churches, the back door has been open wider than the front door. In other words, more people have dropped out than have joined. We see this in a decline in attendance, members, mission involvement, and baptisms.

At the same time, plans for discipling or leadership development for those involved were all but abandoned. Churches have experienced leadership erosion. For years, Bible study group leaders enlisted teams to assist adult teachers. Apprentice teachers, friend care leaders, and member care leaders helped teachers carry out the work of teaching, reaching, and caring. These group care teams met together, set goals, and held one another accountable to carry out that work.

Thus, our groups grew in number and in care. At the same time, needed church leaders were trained in the safe environment of group ministry. Some of these leaders were noted for good character and example, becoming the next generation of deacons, group leaders, committee members, and others.

Too often in recent years, no expectations have been made for group leaders to enlist a team. Since teamwork requires more time in the short run, many failed to fill vacant roles, and they became responsible for all the teaching, reaching, and caring. Busy group leaders tended to neglect reaching and caring. Overwhelmed with the work required, they burned out and bailed out. And at the same time, no trained replacements were in the wings. This leadership vacuum produced a leadership implosion.

These leadership shortfalls impact the state of the Bible study experience. Without a leadership team to assist the teacher, he or she finds it difficult to focus effectively on teaching. When he or she does focus on teaching, guilt emerges because some members are not cared for and friends are not reached.

With no training, few understand how to prepare well and the importance of involvement by the group. While some leaders are self-starters who strive to improve on their own, many are not. Some have a daily relationship with our Lord, but others rest on a past experience with Him. These deficiencies produce frustrating Bible study experiences.

God and His people deserve our best efforts. Nothing less will do. What steps should we take to restore the creation of life-changing experiences in God's Word? How can we overcome neglect and barriers to make disciples of all nations?

This book is designed to elevate your vision and help you understand practical solutions and steps. Get out a highlighter and a pen. Highlight important points as you read. Record ideas, questions, and comments from each chapter. The time spent reflecting on each chapter, your adjustments, and your strategy for improvement can change lives, beginning with your own.

Refer to the appendices. Pray over discoveries and insights and share them with a friend. Study the book together and determine needs and priorities. Hold one another accountable to improve and add deadlines to your calendar. Enlist a leadership team and make assignments. Give God and His people your best; they deserve no less.

Meeting God in Bible study can be life and world changing! First, your own personal spiritual growth brings a fresh relationship with God, His Word, and those He has entrusted to you. Second, your students' encounter with God in His Word will strengthen their relationship with God, His Word, and you. Third, as you grow as a disciple and go forth individually and as a group, the world is changed because of the Lord you serve and the difference He makes in your life. Sounds a lot like Acts 2, doesn't it?

As you begin this journey, my prayer for you is the benediction from Hebrews 13:20-21:

> *Now may the God of peace . . . equip you with all that is good to do His will, working in us what is pleasing in His sight, through Jesus Christ. Glory belongs to Him forever and ever. Amen.*

PART ONE

THE FIRST ENCOUNTER

REVOLUTIONARY BATTLE OF SARATOGA

The British war strategy was for General Burgoyne to march south along the Hudson River to Albany while General Howe moved north along the river. The goal was to split New England and end the war. Instead, Howe sailed down to the Chesapeake and up toward Pennsylvania to take Philadelphia.

Instead of meeting Howe at Saratoga with reinforcements, the Royal army was driven back toward Canada in a series of battles with Benedict Arnold, Nathanael Greene, and company. Burgoyne felt he had to press on to Albany, but the American army was blocking his way at Bemis Heights.

The British made a couple of failed attempts to break through American defenses. Eventually they withdrew to Saratoga and were surrounded by American troops. The depleted British army was forced to surrender in October 1777. With a fourth of the British forces on colonial soil captured, American independence was all but assured.

CHAPTER 1

NEGLECT OF THE FIRST ENCOUNTER

Britsh plans failed in part because of a lack of coordination. The expected reinforcements never arrived, so the desired outcome was jeopardized. Many Bible study plans fail for the same reason. God has big plans for a lesson to change lives, but if the teacher misses the first meeting, an encounter with God, the truth of God's Word does not impact the teacher, and the lesson lacks life and power. Life change for the teacher and the group was the plan, but busyness and "warm fuzzies" were the result.

On the pages that follow, when I refer to Bible study groups, I include both small groups and Sunday School classes (whether at home, church, or another location). Hundreds of books have been written about teaching Bible study groups. Most have focused on the need for, benefits of, and methods for personal Bible study and lesson preparation. But in this book, I want to encourage two paradigm shifts in our thinking. Both focus on the first and the second encounters. Let's start with the first encounter.

What, then, is the first encounter? The first encounter is the time the teacher sets aside to meet God in Bible study, the teacher's personal experience of encountering God and being changed because of the experience. While it can happen during lesson preparation, that personal time with God is more important than the lesson itself.

When I refer to the teacher, I am describing the leader responsible for facilitating the group's Bible study experience. For the teacher, time with God *is* the lesson. God uses the first encounter to impact the teacher and prepare him or her to guide others to discover the truth of His Word. The teacher can then prepare to help learners hear and obey. The first encounter is that critical.

How, then, does neglect of the first encounter happen? Some teachers respond to a need or fill a position. They are drafted (or pressured) in the halls of the church without praying about the opportunity. They are handed a leader book and maybe a list of names. Many of these teachers have little understanding of how to prepare or why it is important to meet God in Bible study.

Some have never been taught how to study God's Word for themselves. All they know about teaching is what they have observed. In these cases, is it any wonder that the first encounter is neglected?

While these teachers are not to blame for how they were enlisted, they are responsible for connecting with God prior to teaching. When they fail to do so, they share the blame with those who enlisted them. Sadly, those who simply *fill a position* can prevent a passionate, God-called individual from filling that role.

For other teachers, neglect is not intentional. They responded to God's call to teach. They love God and spending time in His Word. They enjoy the people they teach. They begin well. They spend hours preparing. People are touched, and lives are changed. Then, something happens either suddenly due to life circumstances or slowly over a long time.

SUDDEN LIFE CIRCUMSTANCES

Some life events contribute to neglect of personal time with God and decreased preparation. In other words, these circumstances cause an unforeseen change for some individuals. Consider the following examples of things that can get in the way of this first encounter:

- personal illness
- illness of a family member requiring additional care
- working longer hours
- insomnia with stress
- work schedule change or starting a second job
- loss of a job causing a job search, move, and/or loss of self-esteem
- childbirth and all the inherent interruptions
- loss of a loved one
- starting college and adjusting to the demands
- fire or other natural disasters

These circumstances do not always impact the first encounter, but commitment to teaching effectiveness can waver. Teachers can lose their focus, as time becomes difficult to manage. The drain on energy can make thinking and wise choices more difficult.

GRADUAL CHANGE

In addition to sudden changes, the first encounter for many other teachers is impacted slowly over a long time. These teachers start out with great intentions and energy. They can hardly wait to meet God during prayer and Bible study and spend a large amount of time in God's Word. Personal impact by God in His Word is great, as they invest heavily in study and preparation, fueling excitement in the group time.

And then it begins. Perhaps the excitement and newness wears off because of the effort required. Enjoyment is exchanged for dread at the thought of another lesson coming. Life has a way of filling a person's available time plus more and over weeks or months, anticipation of meeting God decreases. Less time is devoted to preparing well, and guilt and regret set in. Preparation becomes rushed. Reliance upon past knowledge becomes the norm rather than a dependence on a fresh word from God. Excitement is rare.

Many teachers finish one lesson with a private commitment to do a better job in the coming week. Unexpected interruptions intrude. Before the teacher knows it, the night before the group's meeting has come again, and a lesson must be prepared.

At that point, the teacher has little time to invest in meeting God and has missed illustrations God provided throughout the week. The teacher creates another hastily prepared lecture. Lessons are no longer life-changing; they become just good enough. Without the first encounter with God, the teacher is unprepared to lead a life-changing, second encounter.

Instead of the teacher being changed through the encounter, he or she simply completes a quick content cram course. By skimping on the first encounter, the teacher stops growing and so does the group. He or she stops teaching *from* personal life change *for* the purpose of life change in learners. When the teacher merely prepares a lesson without letting God and His Word impact his or her life, he or she is ill-prepared to serve as a guide to meet God in the passage for the day.

NEGLECT OF RELATIONSHIPS

Besides neglecting this personal encounter with God, many teachers fail to spend time getting to know attenders. They spend time with them only for group meetings. Much of that time is invested with a group rather than with individuals. These teachers rush to group time, usually arriving late, and rush out of the group as soon as the lesson is over, relieved to have survived another week. This allows little time for interaction outside of teaching time.

They make no visits to homes or appointments to meet with group members or friends. These teachers assume they know enough about the group to teach well, but because they don't know these individuals personally, they are hindered in their first encounter preparation time and plan a generic lesson with little impact because the target is too broad. Rather than preparing a lesson that focuses on real issues in the lives of attenders, the lesson brings more agreement than conviction.

LEARNING STYLE PREFERENCE

Many teachers fail to discover and understand attenders' learning styles and needs. These teachers lean toward exclusive use of lecture or discussion, both verbal methods. Lecture and discussion are good methods, but they may lead to a learning disconnect since almost 65% of society are visual learners today.[2] Besides visual and verbal learners, others may be kinetic learners, people who learn by doing.

When a teacher neglects the learning-style preferences, the teaching is not as effective. Learners retain less of what is taught and are less interested. The intended result of a life change fails to occur. Attenders struggle to apply what they cannot remember.

In summary, teachers neglect the first encounter for a variety of reasons. Few do so intentionally, but sudden life events and long-term decline do take their toll. Without the proper motivation and prioritization, the teacher has less time for God to change his or her life. The teacher then spends less time getting to know learners and their learning styles. Thus, lessons and life change limp along.

Revolutionary Bible study groups demand more. The chapters ahead offer solutions that may be a paradigm shift for many, but when we realize why change is needed, the question becomes where to start. Let's discover those answers together.

---

2   Patricia Vakos, "Why the Blank Stare? Strategies for Visual Learners," *www.phschool.com/eteach/social_studies/2003_05/essay.html*, (January 16, 2017).

CHAPTER 2

GOD'S WORD AND THE FIRST ENCOUNTER

God has a great deal to say about how He speaks through His Word. The following passages are but a few to consider. They give a taste of the importance of the first encounter.

These passages are in the order in which they are found in the Bible rather than per content or priority. Consider these Scriptures in the context of neglect of the first encounter:

STILL SMALL VOICE

God does not force Himself on people. He is present on the good days and the challenging ones. Elijah struggled to understand this lesson.

> *And he said, Go forth, and stand upon the mount before the Lord. And, behold, the Lord passed by, and a great and strong wind rent the mountains, and brake in pieces the rocks before the Lord; but the Lord was not in the wind: and after the wind an earthquake; but the Lord was not in the earthquake: And after the earthquake a fire; but the Lord was*

not in the fire: and after the fire a still small voice.
(1 Kings 19:11-12 KJV)

I participated in a team-building activity in which participants paired off. One member of the pair was blindfolded and told not to speak. The blindfolded group was then led into a room with several obstacles in place. The seeing partner attempted to verbally instruct his or her blindfolded partner how to cross the room while avoiding the obstacles. All other seeing partners were trying to help their blindfolded partners at the same time. It quickly became loud and confusing.

Successful partners learned to communicate without yelling. As the blindfolded partner had to focus on listening for his or her partner's voice, the seeing partner learned to give simple and clear instructions. Trust was essential.

God speaks, but too often we are focused on the sound of the wind, rocks, and earthquake. We fill our days with noise and leave little silence to hear God. Moving from a neglected first encounter to a revolutionary one requires intentional listening.

DEVOTION TO STUDY AND OBSERVANCE

Now Ezra had determined in his heart to study the law of the LORD, obey it, and teach its statutes and ordinances in Israel. (Ezra 7:10)

Ezra did more than prepare to teach. He prepared himself to know the Law and to practice it, which makes every teacher more believable. When life and word agree, trust is developed, and the teacher is more likely to influence the learner.

Passion matters. People can tell when a teacher is passionate about God and His Word. They can tell when a lesson has struck a chord and when a teacher believes what he or she is teaching. This experience begins when the teacher has a deep personal desire to know Him, His Word, His ways, and His will.

As a teacher, a passionate desire to teach others what you've experienced grows. The Bible says Ezra *devoted himself* (NIV). He set his heart and mind on study, observance, and teaching. He was determined. Nothing was going to get in his way. What do you need to do to ensure your devotion to Him through study, observation, and teaching? How can you make it a priority and keep your commitment?

HIDDEN IN MY HEART

The psalmist wrote some important words about letting God's Word seep into who we are. He shared some practices that helped him overcome temptation.

I have treasured Your word in my heart so that I may not sin against You.

LORD, may You be praised; teach me Your statutes.

With my lips I proclaim all the judgments from Your mouth.

I rejoice in the way revealed by Your decrees as much as in all riches.

I will meditate on Your precepts and think about Your ways.

I will delight in Your statutes; I will not forget Your word. (Ps. 119:11-16)

Many good Bible study preparation practices are packed into these few words. Meditating on, memorizing, and learning Scripture is valuable. I might not be able to read a Bible while driving, but I can always have God's Word with me when it has been memorized.

And when I need Scripture for teaching, sharing, or personal conviction, it will be available. God's Word enables us to know how to live so our lives are acts of worship filled with praise and thanksgiving. Meditation leads to understanding God's ways, enabling teachers to lead others to consider God's ways.

CALL UPON THE LORD

> Call to Me and I will answer you and tell you great and incomprehensible things you do not know. (Jer. 33:3)

God desires for us to seek Him in prayer and Bible study, and when we do, we can be assured of amazing, life-impacting discoveries. He will answer. This should be the prayer of every teacher every day, for life as well as lesson preparation.

RELATIONSHIP, NOT RITUAL

> For I desire loyalty and not sacrifice, the knowledge of God rather than burnt offerings. (Hos. 6:6)

In neglected groups, ritual and tradition get in the way of love for God and mercy. It is important to build upon the past, but Bible study groups must not live in it. God and people are much more important. Revolutionary leaders are careful to seek Him first – in that first encounter. They recognize His presence, power, and compassion. They recognize how awesome God is and their own insignificance by comparison. And they seek Him.

FROM TEMPTATION TO PREACHING

> Then Jesus was led up by the Spirit into the wilderness to be tempted by the Devil. After He had fasted 40 days and 40 nights, He was hungry. Then the tempter approached Him and said, "If You are the Son of God, tell these stones to become bread."
>
> But He answered, "It is written: Man must not live

*on bread alone but on every word that comes from
the mouth of God."* (Matt. 4:1-4)

For teachers to overcome the temptations of Satan, they must
prepare to refute him with God's Word just like Jesus did.
Through handling temptation well, teachers can teach with
boldness – like Jesus did immediately following His forty days
in the wilderness. When sin is in the life of the teacher, teaching against any sin is difficult.

While it is helpful for teachers to be honest and transparent with their groups about their imperfections, yielding to
temptation reveals weakness and brings questions about their
personal discipline and relationship with God. Teachers can feel
like hypocrites, and this makes preparation more difficult since
approaching God is difficult until sin is confessed and forgiven.

SOWING THE SEED

*Then He told them many things in parables, saying:
"Consider the sower who went out to sow. As he was
sowing, some seed fell along the path, and the birds
came and ate them up. Others fell on rocky ground,
where there wasn't much soil, and they sprang up
quickly since the soil wasn't deep. But when the sun
came up they were scorched, and since they had no
root, they withered. Others fell among thorns, and
the thorns came up and choked them. Still others
fell on good ground and produced a crop: some 100,
some 60, and some 30 times what was sown. Anyone
who has ears should listen!"* (Matt. 13:3-9)

Neglect of the first encounter leads to sowing seeds without
intentionality. And while God's Word will not return void,
wisdom is seen in preparing soil to produce a greater harvest.

Revolutionary Bible study leaders are more strategic as they plan lessons for greater retention, application, and life change. They are aware of the spiritual development of group members through time spent together in and out of the group. They know the learning styles, strengths, weaknesses, and how to help each learner take the next steps. Forward progress in spiritual growth is accomplished as more seed is sown in tilled ground to produce a greater harvest.

MY SHEEP HEAR MY VOICE

My sheep hear My voice, I know them, and they follow Me. (John 10:27)

Shepherds often cared for sheep that belonged to someone else. They led the sheep to green pastures and still water, prepared the grazing areas, tended to the needs of the sheep, pursued the lost sheep, and protected them from predators (Ps. 23:2).

To do their jobs, shepherds had to spend time with the sheep. They called them by name. They knew their tendencies. The sheep became familiar with and trusted the shepherd's voice. Even when flocks were mixed in a sheep pen, the shepherd could call out his own sheep from the combined flock with little trouble.

A significant part of the responsibility of the shepherd-teacher is to know the sheep. Time spent together helps build the trust necessary for attenders to willingly follow where the teacher leads, but the shepherd-teacher must first spend time listening to the Lord's voice and following His leadership before preparing to lead the sheep where Jesus, the Shepherd-Owner, wants them to go.

CHAPTER 3

YOUR EXAMPLE MATTERS

Whether you are aware of it or not, people watch you. They listen to you, and your example has influence. Even if you are not a teacher, your example has influence, but as a teacher, it has even greater impact.

JUDGED MORE STRICTLY

Teachers must take seriously the warning found in James 3:1-2:

> Not many should become teachers, my brothers,
> knowing that we will receive a stricter judgment, for
> we all stumble in many ways.

Like marriage, serving as a teacher should not be entered lightly. The responsibility comes with a warning: being judged more strictly – apparently by God. We should consider this when being enlisted and remember it when preparing to teach. Teachers must avoid leading even one person astray with a faulty understanding of God's Word or application of a biblical truth. Prayerful preparation gives Bible study teachers the best opportunity to give God their best efforts.

Your life will often speak more loudly than your words.

When you bring a friend to the group fellowship, group members are also more likely to do so. When they see you sharing Jesus with a friend, group members are more likely to do so. On the other hand, when you teach about forgiveness and your group knows you are in an ongoing conflict with a family member, your example speaks louder than your words.

JESUS' EXAMPLE

Before Jesus called the twelve to follow Him, they heard His teaching and saw His interaction with the crowds. They gathered enough evidence to agree to follow. In your life, what are some notable areas for wise investment in your example?

DAILY QUIET TIME. This is more than lesson preparation. This is daily conversation with God who loves you and wants to lead you. Your quiet time experiences will lead to natural illustrations for your teaching and for your conversations with group members. Since daily prayer and intake of God's Word strongly influences your spiritual growth, your example here is of great importance.

RELATIONSHIP WITH GROUP MEMBERS. Do you want the group to care for each other's needs? Do you want them to provide support in grief, sickness, and need? This kind of caring begins in the first encounter, and then your example matters. Time spent outside of group time with members pays dividends in efforts to build trust, establish vision, and provide support. In turn, that impacts the teaching/learning environment.

LIVING OUT THE TRUTH. Your example of responding in obedience makes an impression. When you share how God's Word impacts you, group members are more likely to recognize its relevance for them. When you share how you adjusted your life in response to God's Word in your first encounter, they are more likely to consider how they can align their lives to God's Word.

FRUIT OF THE SPIRIT. How well do you exhibit the fruit of the Spirit? How loving are you? How easy is it for you to love your enemies? Are you full of joy? Can you rejoice always and give thanks in all circumstances? Are you at peace with God and in all your relationships? In today's fast-paced life, how patient are you with people, traffic, and circumstances? The fruit of the Spirit is evidence of what the Spirit is doing in your life. What group members see in you will validate or negate your lessons.

TRANSPARENCY

Do you put on a façade of never having problems? When you do so, you make your example too hard to follow. In your personal time with God, ask Him to give you the courage to present yourself as you truly are. Your honesty and transparency encourages group members to keep trying. They don't think less of you; they see you as real. Sharing your struggles is a part of your example as a Christian and a teacher.

THE SIGNIFICANCE OF YOUR EXAMPLE

The time you spend with God in personal Bible study, seeking Him and His truth, speaks loudly. When you share how you heard, adjusted, and obeyed, you help group members consider their next steps. They see you as human and responsive to God.

Your example is strong when your daily quiet time shows through – your relationships grow, you take steps of obedience, and the fruit of the Spirit is evident. When your example is strong, you become a stronger guide for a Bible study group. Your group will want to follow, and they will want to follow the Jesus you follow.

CHAPTER 4

SEEKING GOD IN THE FIRST ENCOUNTER

The first encounter is meeting with God before meeting with His people and being prepared to lead them where He has spoken. This encounter is about seeking God and His leadership in prayer and Bible study and then prayerfully preparing for the second meeting.

In fact, every time a teacher opens God's Word, He speaks. Encounters can (and should) occur in personal Bible study, in worship, in Scripture review and memorization, as well as in lesson and sermon preparation. But a first encounter is meant to precede a second encounter.

A second encounter is an opportunity to guide learners into the presence of God through a group Bible study experience. A second encounter is more likely to be expressed in teaching, preaching, or a mentoring relationship. Thus, a first encounter is personal preparation as well as preparation for leading others into His presence. The second encounter (discussed in chapters 5-18) is when you facilitate the group's encounter.

A revolutionary first encounter begins with a living, growing relationship with almighty God. We desire to spend time with Him in prayer and Bible study, and we long to listen to Him and follow where He leads. We yearn to meet God, recognize who He is, and respond in worship and obedience. The psalmist expressed it this way:

> *I will live in Your tent forever and take refuge under the shelter of Your wings.* (Ps. 61:4)

> *I long for Your salvation, LORD, and Your instruction is my delight. Let me live, and I will praise You; may Your judgments help me.* (Ps. 119:174-175)

I am describing a love relationship, like a dating relationship, which embodies a desire to be together, to listen, and to learn as much about God as possible. This kind of teacher wants to spend time with God and is surprised at how fast time passes. He or she eagerly plans the next "date" with God and impatiently awaits the focused time together.

One difference, however, between human dating and time with God is that He never leaves us nor forsakes us. While we are busy with the details of this world, He is there. The relationship can continue to grow between the moments we set aside time for Him. Solomon prayed a similar prayer.

> *May the LORD our God be with us as He was with our ancestors. May He not abandon us or leave us so that He causes us to be devoted to Him, to walk in all His ways, and to keep His commands, statutes, and ordinances, which He commanded our ancestors.* (1 Kings 8:57-58)

The importance of the first encounter cannot be overestimated. Without a teacher's personal encounter with God, the best he or she can do in teaching, preaching, or mentoring is to testify about what was studied. The lesson becomes a history lesson or word study – or worse, merely an exposition of opinion. Life impact decreases or disappears. Connection to God and His power are missed and cannot be communicated.

Jesus reminds us of the essential nature of connection. Lukewarm or partial connection is not possible – it's all or nothing. Jesus reminded His disciples of this important truth.

> *I am the vine; you are the branches. The one who remains in Me and I in him produces much fruit, because you can do nothing without Me.* (John 15:5)

Nothing. Do we really believe that? How many of us try to lead and teach apart from Him? How many lessons have had *nothing* for results? How can teachers keep their relationship with God fresh? How can they prevent burnout and loss of anticipation of time together with God? How can they make sure they are connected to the Source? How can they ensure their own first encounter before leading others through a second one?

The source of a continued, fresh, second encounter is having a great first one. Too many teachers have forgotten what an encounter is like. Some have neglected their relationship with God since the revival, or teen camp, or their profession of faith. The encounter was real with lots of impact, but memories of old encounters are never as impactful as current ones. What steps can be taken in preparation for the teacher to encounter first?

One of the hardest things for a teacher to do is get out of God's way in the teaching event. The aim is to lead attenders to experience God in Bible study. To do so, we must lead them to hear Him, not just hear us. We must move from serving as teachers of the Word to facilitators of an experience, of an encounter with Him. How can this be done? How can we plan for this to happen?

God created man with freedom to choose, and part of that freedom He gave is freedom to choose or reject Him. When people choose God, He invites them into a personal, life-changing relationship that extends beyond mere knowledge of the pages of the Bible to a daily and continual encounter with Him. That encounter and the relationship that results can be kept fresh through (1) Bible study – listening to God, (2) prayer – conversation with God, (3) commitment – agreeing with and committing to act like His child, and (4) obedience – living as a child of God.

While many may be good teachers *about* God and His Word, few understand how to lead learners to a personal encounter with God that transforms them. One of the problems is that many teachers have never practiced that kind of encounter or had that kind of Bible study experience. The bottom line is we find it difficult to lead others to do something we have never done ourselves.

How can we become teachers who understand the difference? How can we become teachers who serve as facilitators of an encounter?

FOUR STEPS OF A PERSONAL ENCOUNTER

Let's examine the four steps of a refreshing personal encounter.

(1) Bible Study: Listening to God. The first step of a Bible study encounter focuses on two questions:

What did God say in this passage?

And what is He saying to me?

A Bible study encounter assumes a search for understanding the background of a passage. We must make sure that the passage is not taken out of context and look to understand the message delivered to the original hearers. Understanding the message intended for the first hearers helps us apply the passage accurately now. When you open God's Word, He speaks a personal message of truth to you today, and each person may hear a unique facet of the gem of truth because God knows what each person needs to do as a result.

One challenge we face is stopping long enough to listen for His still, small voice. We make ourselves too busy. We fill our lives with constant motion and sound. We rush through Bible reading and devotional to check it off the list, but God desires a personal relationship and has a personal message He wants us to hear and obey. There is a big difference.

If we fail here, the rest of our attempts to move toward prayer, commitment, and obedience will be shallow, incomplete, and selfish. How can we train ourselves to listen to Him? What do we need to do to hear what He has to say to us? How can we lead attenders in our groups to do the same?

(2) **Prayer: Conversation with God**. Leading attenders to listen is important, but relationships, including one with God, demand listening *and* talking – they demand a conversation. God wants two-way communication. A marriage built on one person always talking while the other passively listens is in trouble. The same is true of our relationship with God.

When God speaks, He expects a response every time. When we open His Word, He speaks and expects a reply. We reply in prayer and in obedience. The second question that leads us to encounter God fully (before we lead attenders to do the same) is this one:

What is my response to what God has said in His Word?

Many people separate Bible study and prayer, but these are two halves of a conversation with God. They go together. When God speaks, we have opportunity to respond. In fact, we may each speak more than once in the conversation. We may talk to Him as He reveals to us His truth, one nugget at a time. That conversation will always acknowledge that He is holy but at the same time recognize that through Jesus we are His children.

Because life today has led many to feel time pressures, we rush through time with God, conversation with Him, Bible study, and prayer. Would you rush through a conversation with a world leader? Our heavenly Father is more important. Taking delight in conversation is a key because the more you enjoy the conversation the less likely you will be to cut the conversation short.

Furthermore, a weakness of many first encounters is the attempt to cover too much Scripture. We fail to reflect on God and His truth with any depth. More importantly, when we cover too much, we rush to the end and fail to complete the conversation in prayer. What do I mean? Covering too much usually takes so much time that we rush on and ignore the application of the truth. We need to be careful here: leaving out application, including steps three and four, makes this time look more like lesson preparation than a first encounter.

The teacher sets the pace during the first encounter through personal preparation and prayer. After the first encounter, he or she puts together plans to lead the group to do the same: listen, respond, and not rush the experience. The teacher develops a plan for leading attenders to discover what God said, what He is saying today, and how to respond both during group time and in their private devotions.

(3) Commitment: Agreeing with God and Committing to Obey. In the Great Commission Jesus commanded His disciples to *make disciples of all nations* (Matt. 28:19-20). Then he defined the methodology through which discipling would be done: baptizing and *observing* everything He had commanded them. One of the ways His disciples express that relationship is when they agree with Him, commit to obey Him, and then act on that commitment.

God desires more from His disciples than Bible study (listening to Him) and prayer (responding/talking to Him). He desires commitment to His will and His way. Thus, consider the third question set to be answered in this order:

Am I willing to do what He wants me to do?

What does He want me to do?

If you have been listening to Him, His message to you calls you not only to respond and agree with Him (prayer) but to commit to obey. A commitment is a natural response to God's still, small voice. Teachers determine their own willingness to obey before helping attenders respond to God. Since His message to each attender is unique, the teacher's challenge is to lead attenders to make the specific commitment He desires. Notice that saying "yes" to God comes even before knowing "what" He wants us to do.

(4) Obedience: Living as His child. How does a teacher lead his or her attenders to obey God's commands? The first step is personal obedience. Many teachers only plan to share history lessons, factual content, or moral lessons because they have not allowed God's Word to change their own thoughts or actions. In other words, they miss the step of listening and applying, which is required for obedience. After all, how can a teacher obey if he or she hasn't listened?

But we can listen to God's still, small voice in Bible study, whether in our groups, worship, or personal, quiet time. And we can make commitments in those times of Bible study. In my experience, however, failure comes when we don't keep our promises to God. Too many of us make commitments in a moment of inspiration and conviction from God's Word and then do nothing. Telling God we are going to do something and not doing what we say is called a *lie*. Step four has the potential to change that. In fact, this has the potential to change teachers, groups, churches, communities, and the world.

How can we help ourselves and our attenders keep commitments? We need to ask ourselves this question:

What did I do as a result of what God said?

This may be a strange question to ask at the moment we encounter God in Bible study. In fact, it cannot be answered immediately since we have not had time to obey.

How can we hold ourselves and attenders accountable to keep our promises to God? Two helpful methods include keeping spiritual journals and asking other believers to hold us accountable to our commitments and obedience. These will receive more attention in Chapter 19.

TIME REQUIREMENT

How much time is needed in the first encounter to be prepared to give God and the sheep our best effort in the second encounter? There is no set answer. Every setting and teacher is unique. But with the investment of a little time daily, teachers can meet God in Bible study and be prepared to lead group members on a life-impacting journey into His Word. Encounter God. Prepare to be changed. Prepare well. Prepare for God to use you to bring about change. Enjoy the ride!

PART TWO

PREPARATION FROM THE FIRST ENCOUNTER

REVOLUTIONARY WAR PREPARATION

As with any military engagement, the colonies had to plan to face the British. For that preparation, the Continental Congress served as the government for the thirteen colonies and for the United States from 1774 to 1789. By the time the Second Continental Congress gathered in May 1775, questions were different. War had begun.

Within a month, Congress put together an army for the colonies' defense and appointed George Washington as Commander in Chief. Even with their leader in place, the Continental Congress still claimed loyalty to Great Britain and was not yet seeking independence. The Congress attempted a peaceful resolution by sending King George III the Olive Branch Petition. The king refused the petition and declared the colonies to be in rebellion. With the King's hiring of Hessian mercenaries to bring the colonies under control, grumbling and calls for independence grew louder.

CHAPTER 5

REVOLUTIONARY PREPARATION ESSENTIALS

Preparation was essential for the colonies as they moved forward together to face the British. This is no less necessary for Bible study group time.

If you knew that Jesus planned to attend your group this coming week, how would you prepare? How would you get ready? What would you do differently? Would you take any of the following actions?

- pray more; fast; spend time in silence and solitude
- study the Bible more
- memorize more Scripture
- confess your sins; ask others for forgiveness
- seek to restore any strained relationships
- prepare your lesson more
- plan to teach from the Bible
- clean the meeting space
- challenge every member to be present

- invite every person you know and every person you meet during the week

- make special visits and contacts to encourage attendance

- invite Jesus to teach

- open with prayer

- avoid making announcements or dealing with any business during group time

- check to see if a larger room might be available in case of an overflow crowd

- arrive early

Keep in mind that Jesus *will* be there this week when you gather in His name.

> *For where two or three are gathered together in My name, I am there among them.* (Matt. 18:20)

He deserves your best prayerful preparation. He wants to help you. Jesus wants you to seek Him and spend time with Him during your own personal time. He wants you to invite others to come to Him. This week, give Him your best. Pray. Expect His presence.

PLAN TO USE THE BIBLE

I have seen lots of materials used and misused for Bible study groups. Often, the teacher misuses the teacher's book or commentaries. At times, the group may be using discipleship studies requested by the attenders. At other times, books may serve as literature-du-jour. Each of these methods concerns me.

God's Word is the best focus for Bible study, because only God's Word has the power to change lives. Too often we get further and further from the source. My fear is that God's still, small voice may be distorted or may go unheard the further we get from the primary source – God in His Word.

In addition, teaching materials are often used as crutches for teachers who have not spent enough time with God in prayer, Bible study, and preparation. They read from the teacher book and fail to treat it as a tool that helps them study the Bible during their own personal preparation.

Older children, teens, and adults are able to think abstractly, and they can understand that teaching from the teacher's book is helping them explore God's Word. But there is just something powerful about seeing the Bible in the hand or lap of the teacher as God's Word is taught. Be a revolutionary. Don't rush your preparation. Spend time with God in His Word, and prepare the lesson well. If notes are needed, place them in your Bible. Then, with notes in your Bible, teach from your Bible the next time you teach. Point to the Source for life change even in how you teach.

BALANCED AND INCLUSIVE STUDY PLAN

Teachers who prepare for a revolutionary second encounter lead the group to study God's Word in a *balanced* way. They utilize a plan that enables the group to study the Old and the New Testament. The plan looks at all kinds of biblical literature. The plan is more than the teacher's favorite passages and Bible books. In fact, the teacher studies sections of God's Word that are less familiar so he or she can lead the group to a greater understanding of the whole counsel of God. Revolutionary pastors, directors, and teachers carefully choose a Bible study curriculum that offers a balanced plan, and they stick with it.

Not only is the study plan balanced, it must also be *inclusive*, designed and carried out to include all attenders whether they are members, absentees, or friends. The teacher plans with anticipation that some learners were not present the past week. While plans may include a brief time of review, each week's lesson should stand on its own, in no way dependent upon the last lesson. Would learners benefit from having been in group Bible study last week? Sure. But they should be helped to understand it even if they were not.

The study plan should include all learners whether they are biblically literate or not. While the teacher prepares the lesson with the intent of helping Christians mature in Christ, he or she may also prepare expecting lost and unchurched people to be present. The teacher follows God's leadership and prepares in such a way that the second encounter enables Christians to help those without a biblical background to take steps toward Jesus, making special effort to explain all biblical terms and teach in a way that everyone present can understand.

PACING PREPARATION

What is your usual routine for preparing to teach Bible study? What do you do first? What steps do you take? What do you do last? What is your attitude when you are preparing for a group session? Do you have a hard time believing that it is that time of the week again? Are you dreading the time, or are you just a procrastinator whose time has gotten away this week? Or is your attitude one of prayerful anticipation of what God is going to do this week? Is your attitude more about you, about the group, or about God? This may be the most important question as you prepare.

In my experience, there are several important steps that can move you toward a great encounter, great preparation, and a great attitude. While the following preparation routine is not exhaustive, it can be helpful. For additional information, see Appendix 1. Consider the following (adjust the days for preparing for your group meeting day):

SUNDAY (OR THE HOURS IMMEDIATELY FOLLOWING YOUR GROUP MEETING)
Pray for God's leadership this week. Ask that He show you how the truth of this week's lesson intersects with the lives of people in your group. Read the upcoming Scripture passage (not the commentary or Bible study materials) as soon after the previous Bible study session as possible. This allows the Holy Spirit time to speak to you and illustrate the truth throughout the week. Read the passage several times. Listen to what God is saying to you. It may help to read the passage in several trustworthy translations.

MONDAY TO WEDNESDAY
Begin daily by praying and reading the Scripture passage again several times. Avoid applying the truth to the group here. Instead, consider the passage background and setting with the help of commentaries and other study materials.

Determine the main point or truth of the passage. Look for the author's intent with his original audience. Remain prayerfully open to a greater understanding of the main truth. Apply what the passage says and means to your life before considering its application to your group members. Seek conviction of the truth in your life, and commit to respond obediently to the truth.

THURSDAY TO FRIDAY
Having a grasp on the biblical and historical context and personal application, consider the meaning and application of the passage for people today. Then, begin looking for the difference this truth makes today and in the lives of individuals in the group. What adjustments does God desire in the lives of learners through this passage?

SATURDAY
Develop several critical questions which can lead the group to consider the truth and any significant issues. Begin by reviewing

the questions included in the teacher materials. Adapt them to fit your group. Choose the best methods for leading the group to examine the truth and issues. Put together a second encounter plan, using the plans provided in the teaching materials as a starting point. Gather needed resources. Rest well.

Remember, a few minutes of meeting God in His Word and lesson preparation each day will usually produce better results than thirty minutes on the night before your group meets. Plus, if you start late, you will not recognize the many illustrations God provided for the lesson during the week.

Pray. Prepare for an encounter with God. Pray for life change in yourself. Pray for life change in the group. Pray that God will use you.

TARGETING YOUR LESSONS

When you prepare to teach, who is your target? Are you simply memorizing what is suggested in the teacher book? Or are you adapting what you find in the teacher book to fit your group? The plans you find in any teacher book are there to spark ideas and get you to think about how to best lead your group. Only by spending time with God in the first encounter will you then be able to know how to adapt the plans to best meet the needs of attenders.

God and the church have entrusted you with the spiritual growth of group members and friends. These people (and others who will join them) are your target. These are the people to picture in your mind as you prayerfully prepare your lesson. If you don't know them, then that should be one of your early and regular tasks. This is best done one-on-one or one-on-small group. Invest some time with them away from group sessions. How can you encourage their spiritual growth if you don't know where they are spiritually? How can you challenge them to grow if you don't know how they are struggling?

Without question, God's Word will not return void. But second encounters that change lives occur through prayerful first encounters and preparation. As you prepare, remember to pray for the people in your care. Pray for and prepare to address their needs. Pray and prepare for their growth. Pray for God to work in their lives during the week and during the session. Ask the Holy Spirit to speak to their hearts.

When preparing, focus your thoughts on one or two people in the group. Ask God what they need from this lesson. Be sensitive to specific individuals God lays on your heart and mind. Picture this small group of individuals in your group. Pray over them specifically. Ask God to show you how the lesson can best help them to be obedient. Anticipate their questions and what they might do differently after the lesson.

Then prepare to meet their needs. Prepare so they can take the next step needed. Naturally the target for your lesson should change each week. Address needs of other specific individuals in the group. This focus will help your lessons move from generic to life changing.

NARROW THE LESSON'S FOCUS

Should a group leader push hard to cover as much Scripture as possible in the time available? Or should the teacher spend as much time as necessary to make sure that every attender understands each verse? What is the balance?

It is easy to rush through Scripture, especially at the end of group time or the end of a unit of study. But wouldn't it be better to continue a lesson in the next session so the group can better apply the truth? What if a new person comes into the group in the middle of a unit of study? How much time should be spent catching them up? These questions are best answered before group time in teachers' meetings and in preparation to teach.

I'll never forget teaching a lesson from Exodus 3. At the

end of the session, I looked around the room and could tell the group did not understand the passage or the relevance of it to their lives. I asked them to study the same lesson for the next week. At the end of the second week of teaching the passage, I looked around the room and saw that perhaps one third of the group understood the truth and its relevance. Realizing how important the lesson was, I asked the group to study the same lesson one more week. When we finished the third session, nearly two thirds of the group appeared to understand. We moved on to the next lesson.

Should I have tried one more week? I believe I made the right choice, but that judgment depends upon God's leadership, the truth, and the group. Such discernment of attenders' learning is a valuable ability for teachers and facilitators. Knowing if you should stay in a passage longer should be prayerfully considered.

Whose fault was it that no one got the truth the first week? The fault belonged to all, but my responsibility was to assess and address that reality through preparation and presentation with the right impact.

Most teachers plan and attempt to cover too much too fast. I have seen many teachers try to teach too many verses, making it impossible for the group to understand, retain, or apply any of it. Be intentional in your planning and in your pace. The goal is not to cover the most Scripture. The goal is to lead them toward changed lives.

CHAPTER 6

PLANNING THE SECOND ENCOUNTER

FROM BORING TO EXCITING

Have you heard comments about your group being boring? Do attenders doze off during group time? Do you doze off? Then it is time to add some pizzazz for your lessons – time to shake it up – time to shift from boring to exciting Bible study. God deserves our best efforts and so do His people.

There are hundreds of ways to move from boring to exciting. In fact, the methods are probably as numerous as the number of groups that exist. Consider a few of the following ways to shift your lessons from boring to exciting:

- pray for God's leadership and blessing during your group time to encounter God

- prepare well to bring God's Word alive

- send invitations to regular attenders, absentees, and friends

- develop a theme for the day

- decorate the room

- promote next week's lesson

- contact everyone the day before to ask them to read the Scripture passage

- prepare food

- rearrange the chairs

- divide the group into smaller groups for part of the lesson; pair off for prayer

- use an object lesson

- ask teens to prepare a drama related to the lesson

- meet in another room or location – maybe outside

- do the unexpected

- write a question on a posterboard

- place an assignment in their seats

- give away prizes for answering questions or participating

- ask members to do some research

- make assignments the week before and call for reports

- use pictures, maps, or charts

- use projection technology

- show a video clip (a one- to three-minute relevant portion of a movie)

- ask a thought-provoking question (require more than yes/no or one-word answers)

- share a thought-provoking illustration or story related to the lesson

- use icebreakers

- share personal testimonies

- create two groups and give each group a debate assignment

- ask attenders to write answers to questions, e.g. name five things for which you are thankful

- invite the pastor or a guest speaker for part of the lesson

- ask the group to share what they can do to apply the truth of the lesson

- make plans as a group to go somewhere to practice the truth of the lesson

- give them art supplies and ask them to illustrate what the lesson or truth means

Success depends on the first two in the list. Spend time with God in prayer and Bible study and prepare well. God is worth it and the group is worth it. Lessons that are prepared late in the week and rushed will often bore participants. Don't allow another week to be boring. Make every lesson exciting. Prayerfully prepare to get the group involved. Invest well in the first encounter.

CRAFTING A "WOW" EXPERIENCE

In many churches, worship has grown, but the Bible study ministry has not. Why? There are many potential answers to that question. Consider some of these:

- more energy is often poured into worship;

- leaders in worship may prepare better;

- people may be able to participate more in worship (singing, giving, praying, invitation, etc.) than during group time;

- worship allows people to be anonymous, but our groups do not;

- some fear they will be asked to read aloud or pray;

- members tend to invite people to worship before inviting them to Bible study; and

- attenders may be more excited about worship than our Bible study groups.

Well, how do can we turn this around? How can we make Bible study even more exciting? One piece of the turnaround is making the Bible study experience creative and life impacting. How can we design a group experience that causes members and friends to leave saying, "Wow"? How can we lead them into God's presence so they leave motivated by God in His Word with a desire to apply His truth between meetings? Revolutionary group leaders seek to hit a home run every week. That requires an investment in prayerful preparation.

What are some of the specific signs of a "WOW" Bible study group? Consider the following:

- teacher and members pray weekly for each other and the group;

- prayer time is powerful in group;

- teacher and members know and call people by name;

- friends are regularly present and often return, and many join;

- teacher is well prepared for the lesson;

- the meeting space is clean and prepared;

- furnishings and temperature are comfortable;

- lesson is relevant;

- the truth taught provokes thought and conversation;

- a great opening captivates interest in the lesson;

- teaching methods involve all attenders;

- group members have fun together;

- members and friends can apply the truth to their lives;

- attenders are transparent with each other about their struggles and need for encouragement;

- a real sense of community (*koinonia*) is shared by all;

- caring follow up and ministry take place in times of need;

- members genuinely seek God and hunger for His Word; and

- group shares a sense of compassion and purpose.

RECOGNIZING GOD-PROVIDED ILLUSTRATIONS

What if I told you that God desires to add "wow" to every lesson? God is always active in this world. That is why teachers should keep their eyes, ears, and hearts open for illustrations that God provides for use during the second encounter. In other words, God provides life situations, stories, and illustrations during the week to help teachers and members better understand and apply God's truth to their lives.

Unfortunately, teachers who neglect the first encounter start preparation so late that they miss seeing the connection between the assigned passage and the truth God wants the teacher and the group to apply. To recognize the illustrations, it helps to look expectantly for them. This comes most readily from having spent time with God in His Word early in the week and remaining sensitive to what God shows you. Consider some of the following ideas:

- personal testimony

- family situation

- work problem

- local, regional, national, or international news story

- observation from life's paths

- nonconfidential story from someone's life

Discovering these God-provided, illustration nuggets will further encourage beginning the first encounter early in the week. Read next week's Scripture passage immediately after your group meeting and be alert through the week to life situations, stories, and illustrations that can be used to lead attenders during the second encounter to meet God in Bible study.

HOW MANY VERSES?

There is no set answer to this question. But it would be far better for learners to grasp the truth of one verse and pursue obedience than to study a chapter and apply none of it. Most teaching material includes a focal passage that is no more than a dozen verses. Background material is often pulled from one to three chapters.

Neglecting the first encounter often leads to an attempt to cover too many verses rather than asking for God's help in focusing on one main point. Since most learners cannot remember what they studied an hour later or what the main point was, three or more points appear to be too many.

Revolutionary preparation looks to God for an understanding of the main truth needed by learners. Then all preparation is like a rifle rather than a shotgun – aimed in that one direction. All teaching methods are designed to reinforce that truth. All group activities lead learners to examine and apply that truth. And at the end of the Bible study session, learners leave with a clear understanding of that truth, its relevance for their lives, and a plan for doing something about it.

But this does not happen by accident. It begins in the teacher's first encounter, in personal prayer, and Bible study while seeking God's specific direction. Then the plan for the lesson follows the Spirit's leading and may revolve around one verse or more. Additional verses will serve as context and background for further understanding of key verses, but the target and focus for preparation for the second encounter becomes clear.

INVEST TIME WISELY

Creativity takes times – wise use of time. In *Becoming a Healthy Disciple: 10 Traits of a Vital Christian*, Stephen Macchia states, "Time is the most precious commodity of the twenty-first century."[3]

Wise investment of time makes the difference between neglected and revolutionary Bible study. And the difference between boring and "wow" is wise use of preparation time.

Investing little in Bible study nets little in return. Revolutionary Bible study invests much and realizes many rewards. Leaders who neglect arrive late and leave early. Leaders who are revolutionary arrive early and are not ready to leave when the Bible study session is over.

Relationships continue outside the meeting space. Revolutionary leaders see Bible study as a 24/7 ministry, an investment in important people for whom God has given them to care. Consider these ways revolutionary leaders invest time wisely (much during the week):

---

3   Stephen Macchia, *Becoming a Healthy Disciple: 10 Traits of a Vital Christian* (Grand Rapids: Baker Books, 2004), 123.

- pray every day

- prepare life-changing lessons

- lead encounters with God

- read and study the Scripture

- maintain relationships with each other

- attend fellowship and assimilation activities

- participate in outreach and ministry projects

- equip current leaders and apprentice new leaders

- mentor new Christians

- pray for the lost and members and friends

- meet needs of members and friends

- attend personal leadership training

- evaluate, dream, and set group goals

- focus on and invite friends

- involve attenders in the lesson and group leadership

- listen to each other

- affirm and stretch each other

- deal with problems rather than avoiding them

- hold each other accountable

- adopt or sponsor another group

- start another group

- connect with in-service members (teachers in younger age groups)

- wear name tags and greet members and guests

- make good first impressions
- share testimonies about the Lord and the group
- express appreciation
- mobilize attenders into service for the Lord, the church, and the community
- seek effective leaders

What a list! Today, many leaders look for shortcuts to get the most done with the least effort, but some things cannot be rushed. Macchia also states, "If relationships matter significantly to you and yours, then time is the greatest gift you can give to one another."[4]

That is as true for our relationships with people as it is with God. Jesus emphasized the value of relationships.

Love the Lord your God with all your heart, with all your soul, and with all your mind . . . The second is like it: Love your neighbor as yourself.
(Matt. 22:37-39)

Love is spelled t-i-m-e. Want your Bible study group to be life changing? Invest your time wisely in Him, your neighbor, and your group. Invest in the first encounter. Invest well in preparation for the second encounter. Expect God to bless.

---

4   Macchia, *Becoming a Healthy Disciple*, 123.

CHAPTER 7

PLANNING FOR INCREASED INTEREST AND RETENTION

Teachers need to develop interest and boost retention, but in groups where the teachers have neglected their first encounter, they frequently use one teaching method almost exclusively. One of the most common methods used is lecture, a verbal approach. Teachers may intersperse some questions for discussion within the lecture, but in most sessions the learners are listening to the teacher. This should come as no surprise since a high number of teachers learned to teach by observing teachers who lectured. While many attenders gain some biblical knowledge from lecture, this verbal style is not the preferred learning approach for most learners – from children through adults. This can easily be understood when we recall that 65% of people today are visual learners.[5]

To be clear, some definitions may help. *Teaching methods* are the means or techniques the teacher uses to engage learners' minds and senses in the learning experience. *Learning style preferences* are the preferred means through which learners are

---

5   Vakos, *www.phschool.com/eteach/social_studies/2003_05/essay.html* (January 4, 2017).

more likely to (1) become interested in learning, (2) engage in learning, and (3) retain material.

FIVE-STEP PROCESS TO SELECT A TEACHING METHOD
Revolutionary teachers use this five-step process during their first encounter to select the best teaching method:

1. Meet God in Bible study to discern the truth He wants you to understand and obey.

2. Meet God in Bible study to discern the truth He wants communicated to learners.

3. Prayerfully determine the best methods to communicate that truth.

4. Prayerfully consider attenders and their learning style preferences.

5. Choose teaching methods, which best communicate that truth to those learners.

Most teaching books suggest methods to lead learners to interact with the lesson material. The choices offered may or may not best communicate the truth and may or may not meet the learning style preferences of your group members. Start with these suggestions but adapt the plan to fit your group.

THE FOUR MAJOR LEARNING STYLES
There are multiple learning style preferences through which attenders will become interested in, engage in, and retain facts. Some researchers suggest eight or more styles. Here we will consider four: verbal, visual, active, and rational.

- *Verbal* teaching methods and learning styles involve words, listening, speaking, or reading aloud.

- *Visual* teaching methods and learning styles involve images, whether mental or media.

- *Active* teaching methods and learning styles involve physical movement or involvement.

- *Rational* teaching methods and learning styles involve thinking, logic, or mental exercises.

The following table is not exhaustive and includes only a few teaching method ideas that might be used to address each of the four learning approaches:

Verbal	Visual	Active	Rational
Lecture	Pictures	Drama	Puzzles, games
Question & Answer	Maps, charts	Puppets	Overview, review
Discussion	Video	Drawing	Lists
Singing	Art	Hiking	Problem-solving

All four learning styles will typically be represented among attenders in most groups no matter what size the group is. Each individual has an inclination, or preference, toward one or two of these learning styles. Since planning to meet learning style preferences takes time, preferences of learners tend to be ignored in groups where the first encounter, preparation, and relationships are neglected.

We can discover the learning style preferences of group members in several ways. One is simple observation. Try different methods with the group and watch for those who then become more interested and involved. Take notes. We can also ask the group to complete an inventory of learning style preferences. See Appendix 3 for a sample inventory using these four learning styles.

Consistently using a single method makes it difficult to gain the attention of a portion or all your learners. Often teachers are unable to engage some of the learners in the lesson, and retention is then lower in that group.

For these reasons, along with our Lord's example, a variety of methods should be planned in each lesson. But variety should never be planned just for the sake of variety. It should result from following the five-step process for choosing a teaching method.

When moving from a neglected first encounter and preparation, you may find it helpful to supplement your default method with one additional method each week. This allows you and the group opportunity to become acclimated to the change. Then a second (or a different) method can be added as needed. Then a third and fourth can be added. Taking time to explain why you are making adjustments might also help.

Planning a variety of teaching methods can result in many positives in the learning situation. We recognize that this variety

- enables the teacher to avoid personal boredom through utilization of creativity;

- enables learning to start early by capturing the attention of learners;

- produces a higher level of individual and group involvement;

- increases curiosity among attenders about the next lesson;

- allows attenders to process God's Word in fresh ways;

- produces higher levels of retention, resulting in greater life change;
- enables deeper levels of understanding and discipling;
- creates greater satisfaction about spiritual progress;
- reveals more affinities between attenders, which creates more connections, deeper relationships, and more trust.

ACTIVE OR LESS ACTIVE

Another helpful way to look at verbal and visual methods is to categorize them as active or less active, which can help in planning methods for a specific group, specific location, or a specific lesson. This table shows a few sample methods to illustrate the issue further:

	Active	**Less Active**
Verbal	Drama, Puppets, Making a Video	Lecture, Question & Answer, Discussion, Debate
Visual	Drawing, Arts, Hiking, Creating a chart	Pictures, Maps, Charts, Video

Sometimes it helps to change the level of activity during the lesson to recapture or refocus interest. For instance, the lesson may begin with a less active method and move toward a more active one before closing with another less active method. An appropriate change of activity can result in greater attention and effectiveness.

PLAN FOR PARTICIPATION

Without a plan for leading attenders to participate in the second encounter, participation will be less likely to happen. Many benefits come from involving learners in the Bible study session, because attenders learn more when they do more than listen. Often, the more they are involved, the more they learn. When they say and do something, retention of the facts two weeks later is much higher.[6] And when people are involved in the lesson, they are more likely to feel good about the session and invite a friend to the group.

The following partial overview provides a quick look at major elements in opening, middle, and closing moments of the second encounter.

EARLY MOMENTS

- Pre-session: Design actions/activities before group time begins to focus attenders' attention and thinking toward issues related to the lesson.

- Opening: Start with moments that capture attention and create interest, including icebreakers.

- Review/Preview: Review previous lesson and application experiences; paint a picture of where the lesson is going and why it is important.

- Scripture Reading/Prayer: Pray for God's help in discerning the truth in His Word and read the assigned passage(s), context passage, and/or related passages.

---

6   Edgar Dale, "Cone of Learning," *www.tenouk.com/ConeOfLearning.pdf* (January 4, 2017).

MIDDLE MOMENTS

- Examination: Examine the Bible study passage, context, and truth.

CLOSING MOMENTS

- Application/Assignment: Consider the relevance of the truth for today and for you and develop a plan for applying the truth of the passage.

- Review/preview: Review the main points and the vital truth of the lesson; preview the next lesson and why it is important.

During a life-changing first encounter, teachers meet God in Bible study and plan for the involvement of learners in some or all of the above list. Participatory activities planned for use in the second encounter come in all forms. They can include praying, verbal contributions, help in planning, reflection on the subject, leading a subgroup, subgroup discussion, debate, discussion, reading Scripture, written assignments, drama, asking questions, answering questions, and many other activities.

In planning for participation, the teacher has the opportunity to include everyone without forcing anyone. Since the number one fear for most people is public speaking, even asking an attender to read or pray aloud can be embarrassing.[7] The goal is for every attender to participate in some way at least once in every lesson, so the teacher must be creative in addressing learner preferences and comfort while at the same time using the most effective methods for communicating the truth of God's Word to that specific group of individuals.

---

7   "Fear/Phobia Statistics," *Statistics Brain, www.statisticbrain.com/ fear-phobia-statistics/.*

GATHER SUPPLIES

The message of this chapter and this section is to be prepared. Too many lesson plans are sabotaged by a lack of preparation or by supplies not in the meeting space as expected. Gather what is needed *before* gathering. Go to the church or store if necessary.

If you ask a group member to bring something, remind them the day before. Be generous in your planning. In other words, make sure you have enough. Make sure you have all the resources and supplies needed to make the second encounter memorable, one that impacts lives.

CHAPTER 8

SECOND ENCOUNTER LEARNING SPACE

LEARNING ENVIRONMENT

The learning environment includes the physical, relational, and spiritual environment. The physical environment makes a difference. Some women cannot attend groups due to cold temperatures, some senior adults cannot attend because of the lack of chairs with arms (arms make it easier for them to stand up), and some children and adults cannot attend because the meeting space does not have ramps, elevators, or handicap accessible bathrooms. How can Bible study be revolutionary if people are unable to participate due to physical limitations of the learning environment?

The relational environment impacts Bible study groups as well. If only 7% of communication is from the actual words we speak and the rest is from tone, facial expressions, and body language,[8] how can relationships with group members grow when the teacher lectures to rows of seats?[9] Yes, the teacher

---

8   www.bodylanguageexpert.co.uk/communication-what-percentage-body-language.html (11/30/16)

9   Lucy Debenham, "Communication – What Percentage is Body Language?" *The Body Language Expert: www.bodylanguageexpert.co.uk/communication-what-percentage-body-language.html* (January 6, 2017).

and attenders can connect relationally, but how do you connect with backs of heads? Also, since hearing alone has a low 20% rate of learning retention,[10] lecturing in this fashion might also produce less learning and life change.[11]

Attenders with two or fewer friends in the group are more likely to drop out than those with several friends. Relationships are enhanced when there is interaction between attenders, but they suffer if that interaction is lacking. Furthermore, those who drop out of church tend to cease growing and serving as His disciples.

And we must not neglect the spiritual learning environment. God is at work in the lives of group members, and each has unique spiritual needs. Individuals will often be at different levels of spiritual progress, because some may be spiritual infants while others may be mature, reproducing disciples.

How can we avoid learning environmental stumbling blocks? What do we need to do in our groups to take full advantage of the physical, relational, and spiritual environment?

A variety of dynamics impact teaching, learning, first impressions, and relationships in positive and negative ways. The space used by the group may be too large or too small. The furnishings and equipment available impact the usefulness of the space. The cleanliness, safety, and health hazards in the space are also important dynamics to consider. In addition to these, three A's impact the group: arrangement, attractiveness, and accessibility. Make the most of your learning environment.

ADEQUATE SPACE

When a group meets in the sanctuary, fellowship hall, or a large space in a home or business, the group can seem even smaller than it is. A large space for a small group hinders conversation,

10   http://www.tenouk.com/ConeOfLearning.pdf (11/30/16)
11   "Edgar Dale "Cone of Learning,"*www.tenouk.com/ConeOfLearning.pdf* (January 4, 2016).

causing a negative psychological reaction about growth. When using open or large spaces, we need to plan to help the Bible study session be warm, personal, and interactive. Sometimes we can remove chairs or partition off a large space to make it feel smaller and fuller.

On the other hand, a space that is too small can discourage attendance, because people become uncomfortable sitting too close to each other. It can be difficult to move into learning activities, and temperature can be hard to regulate. Guests sometimes get a negative first impression. These issues impact the second encounter and require prayer, thinking, and planning during the first encounter. Where possible, space should fit a group without limiting growth potential and group involvement.

FURNISHINGS AND EQUIPMENT

If your group sits in pews, the challenge will be to use a variety of teaching methods to meet various preferred learning styles. In any space, uncomfortable chairs make participation difficult. Mismatched, broken, and worn out furnishings give guests a poor first impression and can be dangerous. Equipment and resources should be provided to encourage ideal learning.

However, too many furnishings and too much "junk" in the space can also be a problem. Some spaces are so full of tables, chairs, and other items, almost no room for people exists. Remove all nonessential items. Space for men, women, and children is more important than our comfort from use of tables.

To see the potential, remove everything from the space except needed chairs. Then be careful about moving anything back into the space. Unfortunately, we can become more concerned about our personal comfort than about the space being ideal for learning and the addition of new people. Sharing the space is often necessary and can complicate set up and space use.

CLEANLINESS AND SAFETY

Our space should reflect our love for Him and give guests a great impression. We want it to be safe and present no health hazards. Even dust can present a health hazard for some. Electrical outlets should be covered in areas used by preschoolers and children. The condition of the space should not be a distraction or a danger for learning.

ARRANGEMENT

Rows work well for lecture, but circles and semi-circles are open arrangements which tend to invite more participation. Plus, open arrangements can encourage more interaction with guests and members. Movement into subgroups can capture attention and be a helpful device. Ideally, space should be flexible. Keep in mind, that circles often accommodate as many individuals as rows.

ATTRACTIVENESS AND COMFORT

Help people enjoy being together in the space. This comes more from interaction with God and others than from the space itself, but temperature can make people uncomfortable and unwilling to attend. Make a positive first impression. Decorate attractively, even if use of the space is temporary. Make seating, colors, smells, temperature, and lighting comfortable – keeping in mind that the space is being used for learning.

ACCESSIBILITY

Help attenders and friends find and reach the correct space. Post good signage, and keep age groups together wherever possible. Remember that those who have difficulty finding or reaching their space will be unlikely to return. Where possible, keep senior adult space on the first floor, unless an elevator is provided. Follow laws about placement of preschool and children, and ensure the space is safe and secure. Address special needs, such as handicap accessibility, and continually assess and make concrete improvements.

PART THREE

SECOND ENCOUNTER EARLY MOMENTS

REVOLUTIONARY WAR TURNING POINT: VALLEY FORGE.

Even though no battle was fought during the six-month encampment at Valley Forge, it was a turning point in the Revolutionary War. The 12,000-member Continental Army was desperate – bloodied, diseased, beaten, battle-weary, hungry, and ready to go home. Even George Washington recognized that if help did not arrive, the army was in danger of disbanding.

Several deserted. Disease crippled and death came to many. Fortunately, by February 1778, the weather improved slightly – making life more tolerable.

Then in March Nathanael Greene was put in charge of the Commissary Department. Much needed food and supplies began to trickle in. By April, Baron von Steuben began transforming the troops into a more competent fighting force.

A plot to remove General Washington from power was squashed. By May, word came of military and financial support from France. In June, six months after arriving, a more mature and confident army marched out of Valley Forge, anxious to fight the British.

CHAPTER 9

NEGLECT OF OPENING MOMENTS

L ike Valley Forge, Bible study groups should be an environment where people grow stronger and are readied to conquer the world. Unfortunately, in a group where the second encounter is neglected, much time is wasted. Teachers arrive late. They gather supplies during precious minutes of Bible study time. Members arrive late. The room is not ready. Greeters are not in place. No one takes charge of group business and prayer to help the Bible study session begin quickly. Official start time varies from one time to the next. In other words, the group starts late every week.

On top of that, teaching time is wasted when nothing is done to help attenders begin to think about the passage, topic, or truth for the day. Sadly, too much time is often spent on other activities (fellowship, announcements, prayer, and more) allowing for little time to encounter God in His Word.

POOR BEGINNINGS

Even after the Bible study session begins, many lessons begin poorly. Prayer before the lesson seldom has to do with an encounter in God's Word. In fact, the prayer, whether prayed by the teacher or by a group member, seldom relates to the lesson at all. This is an opportunity missed! Where else will attenders encounter a passion for seeking Him?

And then teachers often admit they did not have enough time this week to study. Such statements should never be spoken. The lesson will speak for itself. When the first encounter has been neglected, the teacher usually moves right into Scripture reading. Or the group takes turns reading verses or sections. Or the group begins to read the learner guide to each other. There is no attempt to follow up on the last lesson or the application of its truth. There is no time given to preview the new lesson or highlight its importance.

LACK OF ATTENTION

When arriving, the attenders' minds are usually on fellowship or personal concerns, and yet nothing is done to capture their attention. No attempt is made to turn minds toward God or the subject, topic, or truth of the day. No questions are asked. No related stories are told. No newspaper articles are read. No summary of the passage and its importance is shared. Nothing is done to get attenders involved and talking early. Too often, one voice tends to dominate those early moments – that of the teacher.

NO BIBLES

Worse yet, the Bible is often absent. Sometimes even the teachers fail to bring one, so they read directly from the teaching book rather than God's Word and prepared notes. Without the example of the teacher and any expectation, fewer and fewer attenders bring their own Bibles. And if they do bring their Bibles, they often fail to open them. When the second encounter is neglected like this, is it any wonder that Christians are biblically illiterate, lives are not changed, members don't stay, and new people are not reached? If we fail to teach them how to use the Bible during time together as a group, will attenders be able to do so daily?

CHAPTER 10

GOD'S WORD ON TEACHING

God's Word from Genesis to Revelation is filled with stories about people leading others to encounter God. This is the second encounter – when one individual who has already encountered God leads others to meet Him. The people leading these encounters range from Moses to priests, prophets to kings, Jesus to Paul, and many more. In addition to these stories, there are many passages about teaching. Consider the following passages as they are applied to the opening moments of the second encounter.

JESUS AS TEACHER

One of the most common names Jesus affirmed for Himself was rabbi or teacher.

> *You call Me Teacher and Lord. This is well said, for I am.* (John 13:13)

Jesus was a teacher of large groups, small groups, and individuals. He made people think in new ways about God and the kingdom. Jesus brought fresh understanding and life change. He did not teach as others taught.

When Jesus had finished this sermon, the crowds
were astonished at His teaching, because He was
teaching them like one who had authority, and not
like their scribes. (Matt. 7:28-29)

Jesus' life and teaching serve as vital content for those who teach Bible study. He left His followers with a mission, expecting them to baptize and teach others to observe everything He commanded (Matt. 28:20). Like Jesus, revolutionary Bible study teachers choose to lead people to a deeper understanding of God, His will, and His ways, and then toward obedience.

TEACHING AS A GIFT

Paul listed teaching as a spiritual gift.

According to the grace given to us, we have different
gifts: If prophecy, use it according to the standard
of one's faith; if service, in service; if teaching, in
teaching; if exhorting, in exhortation; giving, with
generosity; leading, with diligence; showing mercy,
with cheerfulness. (Rom. 12:6-8)

Those with the gift of teaching should use that gift to build up the church, but the gift of teaching is not the only spiritual gift that can be useful in serving as a Bible study teacher. Two of the most important things that a teacher can bring to the second encounter are a call from God to serve as a teacher and a fresh first encounter with God in His Word. These two things bring passion that can be used in the second encounter by teachers regardless of their giftedness.

HOLY SPIRIT AS TEACHER

The Spirit has an important role in teaching.

But the Counselor, the Holy Spirit – the Father will

*send Him in My name – will teach you all things and
remind you of everything I have told you.* (John 14:26)

A revolutionary Bible study teacher never stops learning. He/
she remains open and sensitive to the Holy Spirit, which is as
vital in the first encounter as it is in leading the group during
the second encounter. Learners will understand so much more
of God's Word and Jesus' teaching when they listen to the Spirit.
The early moments of the second encounter are critical as the
teacher leads the group to acknowledge the presence and work
of the Spirit.

EXAMPLE AND INTEGRITY OF THE TEACHER

The example of the teacher in and beyond the group has power
to teach and encourage. Transparency has a greater impact
than perfection because some learners can be intimidated
by teachers who appear never to struggle or stumble. But the
impact of words is lessened when the example counters the
words. The importance of the teacher's example can be found
throughout the New Testament. Consider these four passages
from Paul's writings.

> *You then, who teach another, don't you teach your-*
> *self? You who preach, "You must not steal"—do you*
> *steal? You who say, "You must not commit adultery"*
> *—do you commit adultery? You who detest idols, do*
> *you rob their temples?* (Rom. 2:21-22)

When sin exists in the life of the teacher, attenders (especially
youth and adults) often fail to take the teacher seriously. Besides
that, attenders struggle with believing that a teacher who has
not dealt with sin can enter God's presence to prepare or lead
them to do so.

> *Let no one despise your youth; instead, you should*
> *be an example to the believers in speech, in conduct,*

in love, in faith, in purity. Until I come, give your
attention to public reading, exhortation, and teach-
ing. Do not neglect the gift that is in you; it was
given to you through prophecy, with the laying on of
hands by the council of elders. (1 Tim. 4:12-14)

Age and maturity are not always equal. Example at any age
is essential for the teacher. When speech, life, love, faith, and
purity are positive, a powerful platform is present for influenc-
ing the behavior and lives of learners. Such a platform helps
attenders be willing to follow the leadership of the teacher. And
in turn, the teacher can lead learners to enter God's presence
in Bible study and be open to Him and the change necessary
to be His people.

But you have followed my teaching, conduct, purpose,
faith, patience, love, and endurance, along with the
persecutions and sufferings . . . But as for you, con-
tinue in what you have learned and firmly believed.
You know those who taught you, and you know that
from childhood you have known the sacred Scriptures,
which are able to give you wisdom for salvation
through faith in Christ Jesus. (2 Tim. 3:10-11, 14-15)

When teachers are honest about their struggles with their
group, learners won't think less of them. Instead, they will
consider their teachers to be approachable and real. They will
tend to believe their teaching even more. The ability to enter
the second encounter depends upon the trust and confidence
established between the teacher and the group.

Make yourself an example of good works with integ-
rity and dignity in your teaching. Your message is to
be sound beyond reproach, so that the opponent will
be ashamed, having nothing bad to say about us.
(Titus 2:7-8)

Teaching with integrity reduces fear of being "caught," criticized, or condemned. Even when facing criticism, a teacher who is a model can stand tall. This leads to sheep who are willing to follow even in the face of unjust criticism, knowing they can trust the teacher.

PASSION FOR LEARNING

New believers and long-term believers should be devoted to learning more about God's Word.

> So those who accepted his message were baptized, and that day about 3,000 people were added to them. And they devoted themselves to the apostles' teaching, to the fellowship, to the breaking of bread, and to the prayers. (Acts 2:41-42)

The early believers *devoted themselves to* the kinds of experiences that make up holistic, life-changing Bible study experiences. They were devoted to seeking God in His Word and in prayer. They invested in relationships and fellowship with each other. When this devotion is present in a Bible study group, attenders naturally desire God to intersect their lives, to break into their groups, and to speak to them personally. Teachers must foster this expectation every time the group gathers.

STRICTER JUDGMENT

The teacher always learns more from preparation and presentation of the lesson than the attenders, but the teacher must enter any teaching time with a bit of fear and trepidation. The words of James should drive a teacher to his or her knees prior to and during the second encounter.

> Not many should become teachers, my brothers, knowing that we will receive a stricter judgment, for we all stumble in many ways. (James 3:1-2)

The other participant for the second encounter, like the first encounter, is God. This is true for the teacher and for attenders. When a teacher dedicates his or her efforts to God, inadequacies are always recognized, but a higher expectation about giving God the best effort possible in leading learners toward an encounter with Him is also present.

GOD'S WORD IS PROFITABLE

Do you value God's Word? Does your group? Then you will recognize the benefit of teaching and learning from God's Word. While commentaries, teacher and pupil books, and devotionals are helpful, you will want to go to the Bible. You will want to invest regular time with God in Bible study. And you will want to lead your group to do the same.

Paul encouraged a young preacher by reminding him of the importance of Scripture.

> *All Scripture is inspired by God and is profitable for teaching, for rebuking, for correcting, for training in righteousness, so that the man of God may be complete, equipped for every good work.* (2 Tim. 3:16-17)

Paul reminded Timothy that life change takes place through a combination of teaching, rebuking, correcting, and training in righteousness. Permanent life change demands more than personal determination; it requires the Holy Spirit's work within us. Scripture helps each of us become complete and equipped.

In a group, life change is best facilitated when learners are led to encounter God in His Word. That is where they meet an awesome God and realize their own inadequacies. They recognize the love of a Savior as well as their need to change with supportive encouragers. They learn to love Him, others, and self. They are now able to do *every good work*, whatever He calls them to do.

Bible study groups are equipping centers for Christians, a family of believers who prepare and send group members out as ministers and missionaries. The second encounter is a great time to help group members value the Bible, to raise expectations, and to prepare them for what God wants to do in their lives.

The early moments of a second encounter can be critical for creating an expectation of the outcome. This happens both through sharing ways attenders applied last week's truth as well as by identifying the importance and relevance of this week's lesson. And it continues as the truth is applied in the lives of attenders who are led to respond in obedience. To create this expectation, the teacher must also have insight into what God's Word says about teaching in the middle and closing moments.

TEACHING IN MIDDLE MOMENTS
JESUS' MODEL OF DISCIPLING

The church should do everything according to Jesus' teaching and example. I hear objections frequently that Bible study groups cannot accomplish discipling. When we expect nothing or very little from our groups, we will likely get just that – little and nothing. Jesus showed us how to make disciples.

> *Then He went up the mountain and summoned those He wanted, and they came to Him.* (Mark 3:13)

> *Now He was going around the villages in a circuit, teaching.*

> *He summoned the Twelve and began to send them out in pairs.* (Mark 6:6-7)

> *The apostles gathered around Jesus and reported to Him all that they had done and taught.* (Mark 6:30)

Jesus' example here of discipling included four steps:

1. He called to Himself those He wanted to disciple.

2. He allowed them to observe and learn from His life *and* teaching.

3. He sent them out in pairs when they were ready to do what He had been doing.

4. He called them together to report what happened.

A Bible study group that plans to impact lives must include each of the four steps of Jesus' discipling model: (1) pray and invite, (2) model and teach, (3) send, and (4) report.

TO PRESENT EVERYONE MATURE IN CHRIST

Movement toward life change is more likely when teachers lead attenders to encounter God in His Word.

> *We proclaim Him, warning and teaching everyone with all wisdom, so that we may present everyone mature in Christ.* (Col. 1:28)

The gospel message is about Jesus. The possibility of a restored relationship with God is because of Jesus. The goal is to lead attenders to Him and then to maturity in Him. This comes from understanding the Word, Jesus' life and teaching, and how we can live like Him today. The teacher leading a life-changing second encounter understands and pursues that goal.

No lesson is taught for the sake of filling an hour or making attenders feel good. Lessons may affirm, challenge, and even be difficult. The second encounter is an opportunity for reflection, evaluation, conviction, confession, and repentance. The teacher cannot make attenders mature, but he or she can provide time in the Word, so attenders can encounter God and discover His expectations for their lives. The best teacher serves as a facilitator of a life-changing encounter with God.

PREPARATION FOR GOD'S SERVICE

What is the purpose of those church leaders God has called?

> *And He personally gave some to be apostles, some
> prophets, some evangelists, some pastors and teach-
> ers, for the training of the saints in the work of
> ministry, to build up the body of Christ, until we
> all reach unity in the faith and in the knowledge of
> God's Son, growing into a mature man with a stat-
> ure measured by Christ's fullness.* (Eph. 4:11-13)

Notice that the God-given purpose of these leaders included the
training of the saints in the work of ministry. These leaders are
to live lives given in service to Him and others. Like Jesus, they
themselves are to be servant-leaders who by word and example
lead those who serve others (Phil. 2:5-11).

ABLE TO TEACH

Paul offered clear, straightforward advice to a young preacher.

> *And what you have heard from me in the presence
> of many witnesses, commit to faithful men who will
> be able to teach others also.* (2 Tim. 2:2)

Paul directed Timothy to pass on what he learned from him.
He was to choose faithful and trustworthy people to share the
teaching. But Timothy was not just to teach these *faithful men.*
Instead, he was charged to teach them to teach others. How
does such a perspective change a second encounter?

What if that expectation were communicated early in the
lesson? What if time was taken early in the session to check on
how learners lived out last week's truth? What if, in addition
to learning and doing the truth, learners were challenged to
teach it to someone else? Do you think they would learn the
truth, remember the truth, and be more likely to obey the truth?

What if new Christians were dependent upon Bible study learners to teach them? (They should be!) Don't you think those attenders would pay more attention to what God had to say and how it applies? Don't you believe they would strive to understand the truth? They might even be more interested in taking notes and asking questions. This is a revolutionary shift in the second encounter.

MILK VERSUS MEAT

Does it help when a teacher and a group begin each week with a goal in mind, a direction to head? Does it help to raise the expectation? Does it make a difference when obedience is expected?

> We have a great deal to say about this, and it's difficult to explain, since you have become too lazy to understand. Although by this time you ought to be teachers, you need someone to teach you the basic principles of God's revelation again. You need milk, not solid food. Now everyone who lives on milk is inexperienced with the message about righteousness, because he is an infant. But solid food is for the mature—for those whose senses have been trained to distinguish between good and evil. (Heb. 5:11-14)

Teachers and attenders involved in the second encounter can and should make spiritual progress. But unless they are conscious about doing so, the progress may not be as apparent or as much. Teachers moving learners toward a revolutionary second encounter make learners aware of the expectation and possible steps toward doing so as early in the lesson as possible.

TEACHING IN THE CLOSING MOMENTS

TEACHING OBEDIENCE

> *Then Jesus came near and said to them, "All author-
> ity has been given to Me in heaven and on earth. Go,
> therefore, and make disciples of all nations, baptizing
> them in the name of the Father and of the Son and of
> the Holy Spirit, teaching them to observe everything I
> have commanded you. And remember, I am with you
> always, to the end of the age."* (Matt. 28:18-20)

Notice the phrase *teaching them to observe everything I have
commanded you.* These words are addressed to us as His disciples and teachers. We are apostles, or sent ones. He sends us
forth to make disciples. We teach them to obey, observe, and
do what Jesus commanded.

Teaching them to *know* is not enough because knowledge
alone falls short. Much more is involved in observing, for it
shows our relationship and our knowledge. Observing assimi-
lates and implements that knowledge.

Notice the word *them* in this passage. When Jesus says *teaching them*, He makes it plain that as disciples and teachers, we
are to help them. We carry part of the responsibility.

We are not finished with our teaching when they know.
We are just starting. We are only finished when they are obeying what they know, maintaining focus on Jesus and what He
commanded.

OBEDIENCE EQUALS LOVE

How important is it for teachers to help group members move
from knowledge of God's Word to obedience?

> *The one who has My commands and keeps them is
> the one who loves Me. And the one who loves Me*

will be loved by My Father. I also will love him and will reveal Myself to him. (John 14:21)

Let's look at three phrases from this verse: *has my commands, keeps them,* and *loves Me.* How should these three phrases impact the closing moments of the second encounter?

KNOWS MY COMMANDS

During the second encounter, what is the best way to ensure that each disciple has (knows) God's Word and specifically what Jesus commands? Several things come to mind. Use the Bible. Make assignments. Get learners in small groups. Address learning styles to increase retention. Involve everyone in the learning experience. Review is essential. Allow time for learners to think through and respond to what was taught. Realize that learning does not stop once the group session ends. Ask them to memorize verses. One of the best ways to teach them so each *has my commands* is to lead them to obey Him (see the next section).

OBEDIENCE

We make disciples by baptizing them and teaching them to obey (Matt. 28:19-20). This involves extending an "invitation" during every second encounter, so learners can respond to our Lord's expectations. Prayer together is important. This means we need to lead learners to determine personal action steps out of obedience. Accountability helps accomplish this. Why not ask learners to report in the next session what they did? This could be done with the whole group, in smaller groups, or in pairs.

SHOWING LOVE

When we lead disciples to obey His commands, He is the one being loved. To obey without knowledge is not enough. To know without obedience is not enough. To show our love for Jesus takes both. We will have (know) *and* obey (apply and do) His commands. Teaching only content or knowledge is not enough. The marriage of content to obedience is the loving thing to do.

We must help disciples understand that we don't work our way to salvation. Instead, our love for Jesus shows itself in what we say and do. Every word and action points to the difference our Savior makes in our lives. Love is more than an emotion; it's an action. This understanding impacts how we plan for the second encounter. As we lead group members to meet God in Bible study, we steer them toward recognizing needed life adjustments and commit to move in that direction.

Evaluate your teaching. Are you marrying the two (knowledge and obedience) in the second encounter? Which of the two needs attention for more effectiveness in leading them to love Him? What step can you take this week to address this need?

FAITH AND WORKS

In the natural world, movement, growth, reproduction, respiration, sensitivity, excretion, and nutrition are signs of life. As a Christian, two signs of life are faith and works.

> *What good is it, my brothers, if someone says he has faith but does not have works? Can his faith save him? . . . Foolish man! Are you willing to learn that faith without works is useless? Wasn't Abraham our father justified by works when he offered Isaac his son on the altar? You see that faith was active together with his works, and by works, faith was perfected. So the Scripture was fulfilled that says, Abraham believed God, and it was credited to him for righteousness, and he was called God's friend. You see that a man is justified by works and not by faith alone.* (James 2:14, 20-24)

Christianity is not just about knowledge. It is not just faith. Christianity is knowledge and faith that lead to understanding and acceptance of the work of Jesus on the cross for our salvation. This knowledge leads to obedience, and this faith leads to works. Both faith and works were present in Abraham's life, as James said *by works faith was perfected*. Works complete faith. They carry it out and prove that the faith is real.

The phrase *justified by works and not by faith alone*, calls to mind Paul's teaching about faith.

> *For you are saved by grace through faith, and this is not from yourselves; it is God's gift – not from works, so that no one can boast.* (Eph. 2:8-9)

We are not saved through our works or because of our works. Instead, faith results in works. A restored relationship with God through Jesus is shown through a change of life through works. Works are faith in action, faith lived out.

FRIENDSHIP PROMOTES OBEDIENCE

Why does human nature dislike and resist doing what we are commanded? What if the person asking us to do something is our friend and knows what is best for us? It should be much easier to listen and obey. Jesus is our friend. He knows what is best. Obedience is necessary and good for us.

> *You are My friends if you do what I command you.* (John 15:14)

This verse is set in a passage about loving Jesus. We must do more than *have* love for Him. We must do more than listen to Him. We are His friends when we do what He commanded.

Do you want the group you teach to be His friends? Don't teach them knowledge only. Lead them to meet God every time they open His Word, whether in daily devotions, during worship, or during the second encounter. Lead group members to consider God's point in His Word. Teach them to examine their lives to consider what adjustments they need to make. Even that is not enough. Encourage them to establish an accountability process so commitments result in obedience.

Elevate the expectations of your group in the early moments of the lesson. Let them see the potential result for the closing moments of the second encounter. These moments are critical for life change, so don't rush them. If you want to make disciples, don't skip these steps.

CHAPTER 11

EARLY MOMENT OPPORTUNITIES

R eal change comes from encountering a living God. Some of these encounters happen through life circumstances, and some come through a person, but most encounters occur when God's Word is opened. While these encounters in His Word can happen alone or in a larger group (as in worship), the environment in a Bible study group lends itself well to a life-impacting second encounter.

Many factors impact life change. The first is a teacher-leader who has met God in Bible study during the first encounter from which he or she has prepared a life-changing lesson. This shepherd has an expectant attitude entering the second encounter that is shared with learners and is more common in churches where the pastor and Bible study coach provide training, resources, encouragement, and support for teachers.

A revolutionary second encounter also thrives in a group that prays, enjoys fellowship before group time, and starts on time. In addition, the second encounter benefits from a teacher who creates interest, captures attention, reviews application from last session, previews the lesson, encourages early discussion, uses the Bible, and leads in discovery learning. This chapter will look at the early moments of the second encounter and the activities and attitudes included in a revolutionary experience.

SECOND ENCOUNTER ATTITUDES

In the same way the teacher's rest and personal attitude impacts the first encounter, they also impact the second encounter. The teacher and members will be more attentive, more sensitive to the Holy Spirit, and better able to retain what is learned when they have rested well and come expectant. They will even listen and relate better.

Illness and medication can impact attention, focus, and energy and therefore, can have a negative effect on the encounter. In fact, when one group member is not fully present, the whole group feels the impact. For a revolutionary second encounter, the teacher must encourage attenders to give their best preparation, concentration, and attention to God.

EXPECTANCY

When the teacher and learners expect God to speak and move, they enter the experience with open ears, minds, and hearts. Is there a genuine sense that something is going to happen? Do attenders expect God's presence in group and in their lives? Is there anticipation of God's blessing?

Do they believe Bible study makes a difference in the lives of group members? Are they expecting change? Wanting it? Ask attenders to pray before they come to Bible study, and train them to expect to meet the Lord there. He promised His presence when two or three gather in His name.

One difference between a Bible study group in which the second encounter is neglected and one which is revolutionary is the expectation that something is about to happen. The teacher and attenders arrive with excited anticipation which involves more than fun. More specifically, they expect God to move and speak; they expect to meet Him in Bible study. They look forward to encountering a holy moment, to hearing God say, *Call to Me and I will answer you and tell you great and incomprehensible things you do not know* (Jer. 33:3). Second encounter learners come to the Bible study group recognizing their dependence on Him based upon what He has done in their lives during the previous sessions, weeks, and years.

Not only do teachers and attenders anticipate God's movement, they also look forward to interaction with each other. They enjoy learning and stretching together, even when God convicts and confronts individuals. They know that the group will encourage and support them, so they don't want to miss opening God's Word together. They know something is going to happen, and they all want to make sure not to miss it.

When the teachers and attenders enter the second encounter with expectancy, they are more likely to sense God's presence and hear His voice. They are more likely to meet Him in Bible study and more likely to be open about being changed. They tend to be honest and confessional, realizing their own weakness and need for God and His strength.

With hope and expectation, they know He wants their best. And that expectancy heightens every sense during the second encounter, and they are on edge in a good way. Listening is deeper. Eyes are fully open. The mind is more focused. Memory is crisp. The heart is soft and pliable. God is able to work, and lives are changed.

Lead them to seek Him and His presence. Lead them to expect to meet Him and hear from Him. Lead them to expect a personal message and to be changed by Him.

TRUST AND TRANSPARENCY

Trust is built one interaction at a time. Honesty, openness, and risk-taking grow with every interaction. Trust is built through care, listening, support, and appropriate responses. Some individuals have more difficulty with trust than others. While it can be nurtured and encouraged, only the individual can determine whether he or she is willing to trust the group. Trust cannot be forced.

Trust can be built before, during, and after group time, as well as during socials, projects, meals, and personal interactions. Without trust, the group will stall. If one individual is not honest, open, and willing to risk sharing, the rest of the group may be more cautious. They may be less willing to share thoughts, questions, and struggles.

When trust is compromised, the group will likely be less open to and impacted by God's Word. They may miss His presence and His personal message. In fact, the lack of trust in human relationships often negatively influences a relationship with God, so the issue of trust is important for the teacher and group seeking a revolutionary second encounter.

Transparency builds trust. Transparency is being who we really are – being honest with the group about our positive and negative attributes and open about our needs and struggles. Transparency is difficult without trust, but trust is also difficult without transparency. Both require a risk and appropriate response by the group. Both trust and transparency are aided by the example of the teacher. When the teacher takes the risk to be transparent, to share honestly and openly, group members will be more willing to try as well.

"I HAVE TO" VERSUS "I GET TO"

While leading a conference, I overheard a participant say, "That's the difference between 'I have to' and 'I get to.'" Think about the difference between the two. "I have to" says that the task I am doing is a chore. The person feels forced to do the task and if given a choice, would rather not participate. On the other hand, "I get to" says I enjoy the opportunity to serve. This person looks forward to the task and would rather not miss doing the job.

What a difference attitude makes when doing the work God has given us to do for Him. Read the following pairs of statements out loud. Emphasize the italicized words of each statement:

I *have to* study the Bible	I *get to* study the Bible
I *have to* teach children	I *get to* teach children
I *have to* visit a shut-in	I *get to* visit a shut-in
I *have to* pray for a friend	I *get to* pray for a friend
I *have to* witness to the lost	I *get to* witness to the lost
I *have to* prepare another lesson	I *get to* prepare another lesson
I *have to* lead my group to ...	I *get to* lead my group to ...
I *have to* plan the party	I *get to* plan the party
I *have to* attend training	I *get to* attend training
I *have to* go to a meeting	I *get to* go to a meeting
We *have to* minister to that family	We *get to* minister to that family
We *have to* reach out	We *get to* reach out

If you were honest, which do you tend to say the most? How about your members? Has your service started to feel more monotonous than a privilege? Focus on the difference you and other leaders make and the privilege you have when you serve in this way.

Recognize the blessings that are yours from your personality, spiritual gifts, source of income, and health. Realize what Jesus did for you. When you put things in proper perspective, there are very few things we "have to" do, and there are lots of things we "get to" do. Start practicing the attitude and words, *I get to.* Watch and see if it becomes contagious.

EARLY ARRIVAL

Arriving late usually has a negative impact on the second encounter. When the teacher is late, supplies for the lesson may not be gathered, the meeting space may not be ready, and opportunity for fellowship with members and guests is missed. Time to rearrange the space to prepare for early learning activities may be passed. The teacher's time to prayer-walk the space will be interrupted by a group waiting to begin. Any opportunity to greet and pray with an individual or group before group time has passed.

When members or guests arrive late, their entrance can interrupt prayer, Bible reading, and teaching. That interruption can lead to distraction from hearing God's voice for those learners in the room – whether they are children, youth, or adults. Concentration and focus get lost; preschoolers cry. Adjustments in seating may become necessary. Attempting to "catch learners up" often occurs – at least helping them to know where the group is in the Bible passage.

By arriving late, a less-than-ideal environment for the second encounter is created. To give God and His people our best, the teacher needs to arrive early and should encourage members to do likewise. Obviously, understanding must be granted for guests.

PREPARATION OF TEACHING SPACE

Many aspects of the physical learning environment impact the second encounter, including chair arrangement, lighting, sound, temperature, furnishings, odors, location, distance, and more. Distractions must be reduced or eliminated when possible by removing as many impediments as possible. The teaching team should arrive early to prepare the physical environment because set-up can be even more essential when multiple groups use the space.

Consider the following ways elements of the physical learning environment can impact the second encounter:

ARRANGEMENT
Since 93% of communication is nonverbal (facial expression, gestures, and tone), communication is often better in open seating arrangement.[12] This includes circles and semicircles.

LIGHTING
When lighting is poor (either too much or too little), it can make reading God's Word and understanding nonverbal communication more difficult.

TEMPERATURE
When the room is too warm or too cold, learners struggle to concentrate. Research has shown that women tend to feel cooler and men warmer in a room of the same temperature.[13] In addition to gender's impact, medication and other physical factors can contribute to temperature being a distraction.

FURNISHINGS
Chairs should allow learners' feet to rest comfortably on the floor. Otherwise, chairs cut off circulation and are difficult to sit in for any length of time. Tables take up space and usually limit creativity during the second encounter.

ODORS
Dust, mildew, mold, and odors can be physical problems and distractions. The smell of dirty diapers can cause negative first

---

12   Debenham, *www.bodylanguageexpert.co.uk/communication-what-percentage-body-language.html* (January 7, 2017)

13   Sally White, "Physical Criteria for Adult Learning Environments," *Adult Education Association of U.S.A.,* October 1972, *http://files.eric.ed.gov/fulltext/ED080882.pdf* (January 7, 2017).

impressions for guests. While learners can adapt to odors with enough time, it is often an uncomfortable experience early in the second encounter when sensitivity to the presence and movement of God is critical.

DISTANCE

Distance applies in two different directions. Distance can be the physical space between learners or between learners and the teacher. Too much distance can make the encounter feel more formal and less personal. Too little distance can be uncomfortable and even dangerous.

Some of the preparation of the physical learning environment will be the responsibility of the church, homeowner, or business owner. For groups at church, suggestions helping the Bible study director make the most of the second encounter environment can be found in Appendix 5.

FELLOWSHIP

Caring, interested, and light-hearted conversation prior to the second encounter can help build trust and relationships. Where facilities allow, gathering around coffee, juice, refreshments, or a meal can enable attenders to relax and enjoy the moments prior to the session beginning. Ideally, the teacher would be ready, prayed up, supplies gathered, and the space prepared, so he or she can fellowship during this time as well. Some plan for food and fellowship after Bible study.

Listening is important; being fully present with each other is vital. The moments prior can be a great time to discover affinities, meet guests, and just listen to each other. The relational environment prior to and after the second encounter deserves attention. The group is more likely to sense His care when it is reflected in care for each other.

START TIME

How can we get everyone there on time? People are different; some are people-oriented and some are task-oriented. Some are time conscious and early to everything while others are late to everything. Our best efforts may not change some people's behavior, but in this case, some of the problem could be a leadership issue. If there is no benefit to being on time, why should people show up on time? If there are no consequences to being late, then why should members arrive early?

Why not provide benefits for arriving early? How about offering a meal or donuts and juice or coffee before group time, which ends when Bible Study begins. Could early arrivers have some one-on-one time with the teacher? Could games for children be provided before group time? Could early-arriving adults enjoy a fun activity related to the lesson that gets their minds thinking about the truth of the day? The consequences of arriving late would be to miss the food, fellowship, or fun.

Also, have you clearly communicated your expectations? Behavior will not change if there is no knowledge of expectations. Help parents remember that when they arrive late, it disrupts other children who have settled down. With adults and teenage drivers, explain why you want to start on time. Describe how you use those first moments. Help them see the importance of their example and what they will miss if they are late. Help adults, teen drivers, and parents of younger students see the impression their timeliness or lateness makes on guests. Keep in mind that some guests may arrive late, especially if they have children, while others may show up on time. Some even arrive early, so you must prepare for both.

Calls on the night before to your habitual latecomers may help change this behavior, but new habits often take time to form. Affirm those who are on time and reinforce the concept privately with latecomers. One word of caution: if lateness is only an issue for one or two individuals, don't make it a public (group) issue. Be brave enough to talk individually with the perpetual offender.

How can we start Bible study on time? One obvious answer to getting everyone in there on time is to start Bible study on time. If the group always starts late, no one will pay attention to the published start time. I have often heard the excuse, "I cannot start on time because no one is there." The reverse is usually true. No one is there because you failed to start on time.

Evaluate what you do early. Are people coming to group time in the middle of announcements? In the middle of prayer requests? In the middle of care assignments? Consider moving these to the last ten to fifteen minutes of group time so you can start Bible study at the scheduled start time. Many adult attenders will not want to be late for the lesson, and they will begin to arrive earlier. But remember to leave time to do the other important group business that you moved from the beginning of group time.

How can you get started? Communicate expectations privately if only one or two are late arrivers and to the entire group if more than two regularly arrive late. Consider asking the group to develop and sign a group covenant that includes arriving on time as one of the commitments. Set a date when you want to begin group on time and ask members to arrive early.

Reminder emails, postcards, or a phone chain to all members and guests will encourage timeliness (probably would also gain some absentees). Then, don't back down, because new habits take time; don't give up. A revolutionary second encounter demands that we wisely use the time we have together as a group. God deserves no less.

PRAYERFUL BEGINNING

A natural part of leading the group to meet God is leading them to pray. This is more than prayer for the sick; this is expectant prayer. This is opening hearts, minds, and lives to Him. Prayer is a normal part of the early moments of a second encounter. Some may choose to pray together privately, in small groups, or as care groups (specially formed subgroups to provide member care) before the scheduled start time. Others might just pray prior to the lesson beginning.

Even if announcements and prayer are normally done after the lesson, expectant prayer before the lesson reminds participants Who they are preparing to meet. Either approach seeks to acknowledge His presence, hear His voice, and seek His help. Prayer can be led by the teacher or by a designated leader, but it is too important to ignore.

CAPTURE ATTENTION

Learners come to Bible study focused in many directions: the fight on the way, tasks for work, shopping lists, errands to run, hunger, the game, and more. Teachers desiring to lead a second encounter must successfully direct learners toward God, the subject, topic, passage, and the truth for the day.

Opportunities to capture attention begin before the lesson starts. They can begin when the first attender walks into the room. Capturing attention may include questions or an assignment given at the door, left in chairs, or written on a board. It can include the way the room is arranged, posters displayed on the wall, or the way the teacher is dressed.

For instance, a senior adult ladies group teacher arrived early, trashed the room, walked out, and then walked in with the first arrivers. Those ladies exploded. As the teacher and group members set about straightening up the place in loud disbelief that anyone would treat the space that way, the teacher was preparing them for a lesson about Jesus overturning the moneychangers' tables. She had their attention.

Capturing attention involves appealing to one or more of the five senses of hearing, seeing, smelling, tasting, or touching. A lesson about the Passover meal could include tasting, touching, and smelling the elements. Capturing attention can be completed as a solo experience, in pairs, or as a group and might include meeting at another location. A singles group met at the cemetery on Easter Sunday. During the lesson a person dressed in a biblical costume walked up and told the group about seeing Jesus following His resurrection. The group talked about the experience for weeks.

Some teachers choose to wait until the scheduled start time to capture attention; others start early. They may tell a story, read a newspaper article or headline, or show a video clip. A controversial statement, an icebreaker activity, or a testimony time will also capture attention. Some teachers direct the group silently to read Scripture and answer printed questions, ask questions, review last week's lesson, or set this week's lesson in context to draw awareness to the Bible study topic or passage.

By acknowledging interests within the group, the teacher can utilize that knowledge to include affinities, hobbies, and interests during opening activities. If a teacher knows of learners' interest in baseball, he or she can use baseball images and metaphors. Or, the teacher can ask a learner to compare quilting to the body of Christ.

Many teaching opportunities exist to connect with the interests, affinities, and experiences of learners, but to discover that information, teachers must spend time with learners between group sessions. Attention is more easily captured when building on known interests of the group. And creating interest is an important part of launching the second encounter.

USING ICEBREAKERS

If the group doesn't talk in the first five minutes of the session, they are less likely to do so later, but there are lots of ways to get them talking early. Icebreakers are best done with people in pairs or small groups.

Using icebreakers with a larger group is more difficult. Large groups (more than six people) cause some individuals to hesitate because of their fear of public speaking. But icebreakers can be written activities handed to participants as they arrive with instructions to share with one or two people before they sit down. This allows people to ease into conversation and relationships.

If a group is new, teachers must be intentional in relationship building. Icebreakers help people talk and get to know one another. For the group to go deeper in studying God's Word, they need to trust one another. Otherwise, the study will be shallow and superficial. The lesson will be *about* God's Word rather than a meeting with God that leads to application of His truth. Without relationship development and trust, there will be little personal sharing, a lack of confession, and resistance to accountability.

Purposeful icebreakers are designed to:

- launch the lesson with a hook and capture the interest of individuals;

- bring fun, interest, and a lighter direction;

- relieve stress and nervousness, so attenders relax;

- help learners feel more comfortable with each other;

- encourage the group to befriend and trust each other;

- build lasting relationships;

- allow new people to connect with the group;

- help people branch out beyond those they know best;

- promote comfort in talking and sharing;

- encourage listening to each other; and

- connect to the lesson rather than be a free-standing activity.

When you use icebreakers, plan to incorporate these suggestions:

POSITIVE EXCITEMENT

Make sure you fully understand how to do the icebreaker. Your hesitation or lack of confidence will communicate volumes. Make it fun. Your leadership can make or break involvement in icebreakers.

AGE APPROPRIATENESS

You know your group better than anyone. Be willing to try new things, but remember the past. Consider group preferences and physical abilities when choosing icebreakers. Consider their needs and how the icebreaker might prepare for the learning experience or how it might develop relationships more deeply.

AVOID EMBARRASSMENT

One negative to asking for volunteers is the same ones tend to volunteer over and over. On the other hand, drafting people to share verbally in front of the group can embarrass shy people and those who fear public speaking. When possible, enlist volunteers personally in advance allowing individuals to decline if they prefer.

MOVE ON

Watch and listen in case the icebreaker bogs down. You'll be able to tell by scanning the room. When an icebreaker is stuck, move on. Generally, the key is getting people to talk, so if the room is quiet, give additional instructions, finish the icebreaker, or move on to the next activity.

FINISH THE FUN AND GAMES

Move on at the peak of enjoyment; leave them wanting more. It is better to be too short than too long. Squeeze as much excitement and conversation out of the icebreaker as possible while avoiding the beginnings of boredom.

EXAMPLES

Let me close this section about icebreakers by sharing these three examples:

- In a lesson about 1 Corinthians 13, the lesson might begin with an icebreaker calling for pairs to share about a time when they were impatient in their love toward someone.

- In a lesson about reaching your friends, the session might begin by sharing the name of their best friend in high school and why they were best friends.

- In a lesson about the ten lepers, the lesson might begin with sharing about a time when they forgot to thank someone.

Icebreakers increase conversation and community for Bible study. They are especially helpful in the early weeks of a new group and when new people enter a group. Even long-term relationships can benefit from effective icebreakers. Icebreaker questions or activities begin conversation and enable the group to go deeper in studying God's Word together. Launch your second encounter with a great icebreaker.

REVIEW PREVIOUS LESSON

When a lesson is part of a series, it is helpful to connect the current lesson to previous lessons. Even when this week's lesson is a new series or a separate study, review is helpful. Review can strengthen retention, reinforce the truth that was examined, and give an opportunity to check on application (see next section).

Review can also help learners understand the value of attending weekly, hear what was missed, and catch up with the rest of the group. The review should be brief, lasting no more than a couple of minutes. To keep it brief and interesting, it should be planned. Asking attenders questions about what was learned and what was the point is a good way to capture attention while doing review at the same time.

DISCUSS LAST WEEK'S APPLICATION

An important task for the teacher and the group is to encourage learners to pursue Jesus' directive to observe everything He commanded. A group can hold each other accountable for carrying out the commitments made. The early moments of a lesson offer a great opportunity to ask attenders and returning guests how they did at living out the truth of last week's lesson.

At first the teacher should begin this by sharing his or her experiences, struggles, and victories in response to the previous week's lesson, making this an opportunity for transparency. This will help the group understand that there is more to the lesson than learning truth: obedience is the goal. You also reinforce the expectation that the group will take the lesson seriously in the week ahead.

The teacher can arrange for individual attenders to share the following week, and contact the group during the week to remind them to live out the truth and be prepared to share their experiences. When the teacher leads the group to check on application of the truth, more learners will begin to recognize the importance of God's Word in their daily lives. This practice helps learners listen more carefully to God's Word while seeking appropriate avenues of personal application during the second encounter. Review is also appropriate at the end of the lesson (see PART FIVE).

PREVIEW

Another helpful action in the opening moments of a lesson is a preview. Help learners understand where the lesson is headed and why it is important. Prepare them to know what to expect to help them listen for specific points – perhaps answers to questions, which may be written on a board or on listening sheets.

The preview may flow out of an icebreaker or an activity designed to capture attention, and it may include a story, testimony, or other opening that sets the lesson into context – either in the biblical time or today. Preview heightens attention and listening. Done well, it can lead to anticipation of solving a problem that was described. Preview can help learners desire to enter the second encounter to discover answers for needs in their own lives. It can lead them to want to meet God in Bible study.

EARLY MOMENTS ILLUSTRATED

What do good early moments look like in a group? The teacher prepares well in Bible study, prayer, and planning during the first encounter. Then, guided by the Holy Spirit, the rested and expectant teacher prays and arrives early for the second encounter. The teacher prayer-walks the space, and then greets attenders and enjoys moments of fellowship. He or she gives instructions about a pre-activity, which helps them begin to think about the lesson for the day. The Bible study session starts on time with announcements, prayer requests, and a brief time of prayer in groups of three.

Following prayer, the teacher reviews last week's lesson

and asks for testimonies about living out the truth of that lesson. After a couple people share and a couple of questions are answered, the teacher asks for responses to the pre-activity as a way of capturing interest. The activity served both as an icebreaker to get the group talking and as a preview of this week's lesson. The teacher helps them understand why this lesson is important. Then after these opening moments, the group dives into God's Word to discover what He has to say to them in the middle moments of the second encounter.

CHAPTER 12

FACILITATING A SECOND ENCOUNTER

Which is more powerful: seeing the Grand Canyon or listening to someone tell you about seeing it? While many people enjoy hearing testimonies (and seeing pictures), most would rather enjoy the experience themselves. The exception is when a person cannot have that experience. In that case, we accept the testimony and vicariously enjoy their experience.

In Bible study groups that neglect the second encounter, many are living on the testimony of the teacher. Attenders are enjoying meeting God through the testimony of teachers who have spent time in God's Word for them. In other words, those attending these groups are failing to meet God themselves. They hear about the experience, and that satisfies them. These teachers stand in the way of learners meeting God themselves, being changed by the encounter, and living differently as a result.

A teacher leading a revolutionary second encounter, however, is a facilitator of a meeting with God in His Word. The teacher leads learners to open God's Word and listen to His still, small voice. The teacher prays and prepares well to be a useful guide to the passage for the day and the truth that God wants attenders to learn and obey. This shepherd-teacher incorporates experiences into the teaching plan to lead members and guests to read God's Word, listen to His message, apply the truth to their lives, and plan for a response.

The revolutionary teacher refuses to allow learners to avoid the hard but important work of personal Bible study during group time. No one can be saved in my place, and no one can do Bible study in my place. In fact, many adults today are leaving Bible study groups because they are not making spiritual progress. Leading a revolutionary second encounter is an essential part of helping attenders understand how to be self-feeders, learning to meet God in Bible study on their own.

Keep this in mind. Who is going to teach disciples how to study God's Word for themselves? If the teacher does all the study, the attenders will never learn to study God's Word for themselves. We must not do all the "fishing" for them. They must be taught to "fish" for God's truth for themselves or they will go hungry the rest of the week. When we teach them to encounter God in Bible study, they will own the truth, the method, and most importantly the relationship for themselves.

FACILITATING VERSUS TEACHING

Andragogy is the theory of adult learning methods and techniques with subtle and obvious differences from pedagogy – the art of teaching. One of the main ideas of andragogy is that adults bring life experiences to bear upon all learning. To neglect that fact is to miss learning opportunities, which create many possibilities for a revolutionary Bible study group where the teacher functions as a facilitator.

One reason some churches have difficulty enlisting new teachers is that current teachers give an impression that one must be an expert on God's Word to be a teacher. Yes, teachers should spend time with God in His Word as they prepare to teach, but they do not have to be experts. Rather, facilitators of encounters with God in His Word are needed. Teaching must naturally lead to worship, to recognize the worth of God. Teachers can learn the leadership skill of facilitating to draw out the personal experiences of learners.

This accomplishes many aspects of revolutionary Bible study, including how to increase participation of learners, move beyond lecture, ask good questions, and tap into the relational and physical learning environment. In addition, facilitating a second encounter must be more learner-focused, addressing the real needs of learners and leading them to critical thinking, self-evaluation, commitment to change, action plans for life change, and willingness to be held accountable. The move toward facilitation in a revolutionary second encounter would truly be an extreme makeover of teaching for many groups.

DISCOVERY LEARNING

An important principle of the second encounter is discovery learning. The objective is to send learners on a quest to discover God, His will, and the truth He desires for them. What they discover for themselves they will retain longer, and it will have a greater impact on their lives. Teachers leading revolutionary second encounters want to do more than *teach*. They design and lead an experience in which learning and an encounter are more likely to occur. Instead of teachers *telling*, they lead learners to think, talk, and do. Teachers are intentional guides on a journey to encounter God, His will, His ways, and the truth needed for the learners' lives.

Teachers need to be ready because discovery learning is more participatory and surprising. While the experience is planned with a clear direction and focus, the life-impacting and life-changing results can never be predicted. The response of each person to the encounter with God will be unique. God's Word applies to each person in a different way.

> *All Scripture is inspired by God and is profitable for teaching, for rebuking, for correcting, for training in righteousness, so that the man of God may be complete, equipped for every good work.* (2 Tim. 3:16-17)

Discovery learning works best in an environment of healthy relationships and trust between the teacher and attenders and each other. When relationships are unhealthy and trust is absent, attenders are unwilling to risk. Without risk, steps toward change falter. Discovery learning also requires reserving time for reflection and conversation with each other and with God.

Questions are a natural tool for the teacher leading discovery learning. Those questions require more than yes or no or one-word answers. Here are some examples:

- What are some opportunities for Christians to live lovingly toward their lost neighbors (1 Corinthians 13:4-7)?

- In what ways was Joseph a prototype for the coming Messiah?

- With which of the fruit of the Spirit do you have the most difficulty? Why?

Open-ended questions like these have potential to lead to deeper consideration of the passage and truth, self-assessment, willingness to make change, and decisions about next steps.

APPERCEPTION

In a nutshell, apperception is understanding something new based on previous knowledge and experience. It is leading attenders to draw upon their experiences to make sense of and apply what is being learned. For instance, when eating a cantaloupe, we find it natural to compare it to other fruits to understand the taste and experience of eating a cantaloupe.

In the Bible study group, apperception is more than relying upon tradition or past ways of responding. Rather, it builds the present experience on previous knowledge and experiences to gain a new understanding or simply to make sense of the new learning. Apperception begins when the teacher and attenders draw upon their knowledge of each other, experiences, and affinities. For example, in a lesson about the Lord's Supper, the teacher might invite a member to tell about his experience of sharing a Passover meal with a Jewish family. While apperception is useful throughout the second encounter, it can create additional interest when applied to the early moments.

USE THE BIBLE

For years, I have had a conviction that the church is failing to teach people how to use the Bible. We are not teaching them how to study God's Word. We are not teaching them how to listen to His still, small voice. We are not teaching them how to read His Word in search of truth that needs to be applied to daily life. We are not teaching them how to open God's Word to encounter a great God and realize our insignificance.

While we may succeed in teaching them how to answer someone else's questions, few know how to develop their own questions or how to discover answers. While we may succeed in helping them realize the importance of a passage or a truth from God's Word, it is often not personalized. There is seldom any attempt to discern a personal message from God.

Furthermore, have you noticed how few people use a Bible? With the number of Bible apps available for smart phones, there really is no excuse for a person not to have at least a digital version of the Bible with them. The issue is not the format, but rather the use of a Bible – any Bible.

Attenders who don't use their Bibles at church often fail to seek God's presence and His Word for their lives through the week. Without teaching them to use their Bibles, we may teach them how to do group Bible study, but we often succeed only in teaching them how to follow someone else's agenda in looking at a passage from the Bible.

What are some ways we can teach them during Bible study to use the Bible outside of group time? We once had the "six-point record system" on small pads of paper or on offering envelopes. Bringing your Bible and reading the Bible daily were expected and counted. Some teachers purchased a Bible for every member. Some groups bought Bibles that stayed in the meeting space. Some contests included points for bringing Bibles.

Get them in the Word! Make sure every person owns a Bible, and then don't do all the Bible study for them. Instead, lead them to meet God in Bible study and make assignments for preparation by members between sessions. Divide the group into smaller groups of two to six people. Give them passages, questions, and tools if needed. Form debate groups. Lead them to open and learn to handle (rightly) God's Word. Teach them so they will be able to teach themselves in daily devotions. Help them become self-feeders – to "fish" God's Word for themselves.

Attenders need encouragement to bring their Bibles to group time, so they will know where and how to find answers to life situations between Bible study sessions. Change begins with teachers meeting God in personal Bible study and lesson preparation prior to leading their groups to meet Him when you gather. Attenders also need to be challenged and helped to grow in their private quiet times.

CONTEXT MATTERS
Teachers leading revolutionary second encounters work hard to handle God's Word rightly (2 Timothy 2:15). With that in

mind, they plan and present God's Word in context. They heed the warning of Peter in his second letter: *There are some things in them* [Paul's letters] *that are hard to understand, which the ignorant and unstable twist to their own destruction, as they do the other Scriptures* (2 Pet. 3:16 ESV).

These second encounter leaders must help learners set Scripture into the historical, geographical, character, and writer contexts. Here are some of many questions that need to be considered:

- When was the passage written? What was going on at that time in history?

- Where was the author and where were the hearers? What is the significance of the location on the passage?

- Who are the characters involved? What was going on in their lives? What do we learn about God in the passage?

- Who was the author? Who were the hearers? What was going on in the lives of hearers that called for this message?

This effort helps learners understand the message communicated to the original readers or hearers. Keep in mind that only a small portion of the session time should be spent on the context and background, but such effort is worth the time because it helps attenders translate the message into their own context more accurately. They are then able to apply the truth to their lives and respond obediently.

SUBGROUPS

Subgroups are division of the larger group into smaller units of people to increase involvement in the second encounter. If a group has at least four people attending, the group can be divided into two groups of two.

How many groups and what size groups work best? From my experience, subgroups should be no larger than six people. Nearly everyone in a group of six will participate and talk, and groups of three to five work even better. So, in a group of twelve, create three or four subgroups. In a group of ten, create groups of two to five. The maximum number of groups is determined by what the teacher wants the groups to do.

When groups exceed the number of assignments, give more than one group the same assignment. Call on one of the groups with the same assignment to share their response and call on the other group(s) to add anything they would like.

By giving an assignment to each group, attention and participation increase and in most cases retention does as well. This also is a great method for leading attenders to become personally involved in doing Bible study rather than expecting the teacher to do it for them. Again, while this method can be used throughout the second encounter, it also works well to capture attention early in the session.

AVOID TABLES

I am not always against tables in the learning environment – just almost always. Let me share some of my reasoning for not using tables before I share a few exceptions. Consider these reasons:

- Preschoolers and children are active and need 25-35 square feet of space per child. Few churches or homes have space with an adequate amount of room for these age groups to allow for use of tables, because tables take up a lot of the space that active children need.

- For most teachers and groups, tables limit creativity, the way the learning environment can be arranged, how groups can be formed, as well as teaching method options.

- Tables take up space that could allow for more people, often leading to an artificially lower average attendance than the space could accommodate without tables.

- Sitting around a table can lead attenders to experience an inner circle and an outer circle when more individuals show up than can fit around the table, which produces a negative psychological reaction for guests and latecomers.

- If the group meets around a table, the space might feel full when the table is full, potentially leading to fewer invitations to friends.

- If a group starts with tables and then attendance grows, resulting in the need to remove the tables, most groups become resistant.

- Tables make it harder to transition the space from one age group or purpose to another.

Under what circumstances am I more open to an exception for the use of tables? Consider these circumstances:

- If multiple (three or more) groups meet around round tables in a gym because space in the rest of the church facilities is full (one group per table), tables serve as group dividers.

- If preschool and children's spaces are large enough and have adequate space for current and projected attendance at 25-35 square feet per child, tables can be useful.

- If the group meets in a space that will be used that same day for another purpose, tables may be required for that activity (but why not ask the group to set these up after Bible study?).

Rather than using tables, why not set chairs in horseshoes: semi-circles of four to five chairs. In preschool and children's spaces, teachers can provide lapboards for projects or allow children to work in chairs or on the floor. (Preschool and children's space should not be carpeted due to allergies and difficulty keeping carpet clean.)

In adult space where tables are in use, begin by removing all unused tables. Then, when attendance increases, remove remaining tables to continue growth. Don't allow tables to prevent your group from growing or limit your discipling creativity.

GROUP SIZE

One of the largest groups I ever taught had over one hundred enrolled and fifty in attendance each week. I inherited the group from a well-loved teacher who moved to spend more time with his adult children. It was one of the best organized larger groups I have ever seen. They planned monthly fellowships and organized care groups, and every person who joined the church was invited to the group. Communication was excellent.

I noticed, however, several things that were less than ideal. Some people on the member care list were not known by anyone in the group. Members could be absent several weeks without being missed. Participation in the lesson was by a handful, and there were several cliques in the group. Within two weeks, I began a more interactive teaching process involving eight horseshoe groups.

In my reflection on the group, I now realize that there appears to be a natural limit to the number of relationships in which we can invest well. Since that time, I have discovered some group dynamics research that helps me better understand what I observed.

For instance, in a group of four, there are potentially six different two-way (or two-person) relationships. In a group of six, the number jumps to fifteen. In a group of twelve, the number jumps to sixty-six. The way to calculate the number of two-way relationships (where the size of the group is x) is as follows: [x times (x-1)] ÷ 2. Here are some more examples:

Group of 15: $(15 \times 14) \div 2 = 105$

Group of 20: $(20 \times 19) \div 2 = 190$

Group of 30: $(30 \times 29) \div 2 = 435$

Group of 40: $(40 \times 39) \div 2 = 780$

Did you notice the way the numbers of two-way relationships took off as the group size increased? It has been suggested that the maximum number of relationships we can handle is 150.[14] But if that is the maximum, the ideal number is probably much lower.

Jesus was an expert in group dynamics. He had twelve disciples for a reason. Counting Jesus, that would result in 78 two-way relationships. Since He was God and we are not, His ability was beyond ours.

As groups approach a dozen in size, they tend to break into subgroups (or cliques). This may indicate that these groups should move toward launching a new group. To sustain the group beyond a dozen participants, the teacher needs to enlist additional care team leadership and divide the group during Bible study.

Without starting a new group, enlisting additional leaders, or revising your group care strategy, the likely result is disconnection of individuals from the group. Groups and disciples fail to grow when people are not connected. Make decisions about group size that lead to disciple growth and involvement, especially during the second encounter.

---

14   Christopher Allen, "The Dunbar Number as a Limit to Group Sizes," *Life with Alacrity*, *www.lifewithalacrity.com/2004/03/the_dunbar_numb.html* (January 9, 2017).

BENEFITS OF TEACHING

Over the years, I have taught every age group from younger preschool through senior adults. I have taught groups with only one or two regulars and some with fifty or more in attendance. These groups have included combined-gender groups and single-gender groups. Sometimes I was the only teacher with an occasional substitute. Other times I was the substitute or one of the co-teachers.

In my work as the state Sunday School and small group consultant for Kentucky, I have the opportunity to be a guest in many adult groups, and I regularly participate in a group when I am home. I've been a member of three small groups and a leader of another group. And I have been a member and teacher of many Sunday School classes. That adds up to a lot of attending, teaching, and leading experience over more than forty years.

During those experiences, I have discovered many benefits and personal growth experiences that come from teaching Bible study. Here is my current list:

- greater learning about God and His Word through preparing and teaching

- stronger dependence upon God's leadership

- provision of more materials by the church for lesson preparation

- improved ability to cut off rabbit trails

- greater understanding of teaching methods and learning styles

- improved ability in choosing questions that start captivating discussions

- more input into the arrangement of the learning space, furnishings, and equipment

- more personal stretching and growth through training opportunities

- more knowledge about and prayer requests for members and guests (and their families)

- greater openness of homes I visit

- more awareness of growth of members as disciples

- growing ability to observe growth as members serve and take leadership positions

- more input into group activities and plans

- stronger leadership vantage point for sponsoring a new group

- ability to mentor/apprentice another group leader

- growing relationship with a group that will love, support, and care for you

- better ability to encourage group participation in church activities and projects

- more input into the assimilation process of the group (name tags, greeters, and follow up)

- increased input into the ministry strategy of the group (communication, prayer partners, crisis response, etc.)

Wow, what a list! Teaching has many rewards. Pray. Prepare. Be changed. Teach to change lives.

CHAPTER SUMMARY

Every moment prior to and during the second encounter matters. Group leaders arrive early for revolutionary encounters to prepare the learning environment, pray, and fellowship with intentionality prior to the session beginning. They take full advantage of that time, start the session on time, and wisely use the early moments to prepare attenders to meet God in Bible study. Teachers capture the interest of learners and get them talking early. They often include a review of the previous lesson, check on application of last week's truth, and preview this week's lesson and why it is important.

The teacher leads the second encounter out of his or her first encounter and preparation. The object is to lead attenders to meet God in and through His Word. In that effort, teachers strive for an encounter rather than a lecture or testimony. They tend to facilitate a learning experience rather than teach a lesson, leaning toward discovery learning.

They build on what learners know, use the Bible, and set Scripture into context. They use subgroups and often avoid tables to involve learners in the second encounter. These teachers understand that God's Word changes lives, and that is the encounter with God they desire for the groups. In turn, they recognize many benefits from teaching.

PART FOUR

SECOND ENCOUNTER MIDDLE MOMENTS

REVOLUTIONARY WARSHIP BATTLE AND JOHN PAUL JONES

On September 23, 1779, the crew of the Bonne Homme Richard, commanded by American John Paul Jones, battled the crew of the English HMS Serapis, which was commanded by Captain Richard Pearson. The BH Richard was slightly outgunned. The HMS Serapis was a 50-gun frigate while the BH Richard was barely sea worthy.[15]

When Captain Pearson hailed the Bonne Homme Richard and demanded surrender, John Paul Jones declared that he had just begun to fight. For two hours, the ships were grappled together and did battle so close that the Serapis, unable to open her gun ports, finally had to blow them open from the inside.

With the Bonne Homme Richard sinking, Pearson surrendered to avoid going down as well.

---

15   Lieutenant Richard Dale, "Bon Homme Richard vs Serapis," *History Central,* *www.historycentral.com/Revolt/Bonnehome.html* (January 9, 2017).

CHAPTER 13

NEGLECT OF SECOND ENCOUNTER MIDDLE MOMENTS

Without a good plan, we can take the group down with us. Even with a great start, the middle moments of the second encounter can be full of activities that lead nowhere. These moments can be flat, lifeless, and counterproductive. They can be busy but accomplish nothing. They focus on communicating facts rather than facilitating a discipling encounter with God in His Word.

Despite a great first encounter, what does it look like when the middle moments of the second encounter are neglected? Consider the following:

- The middle and end of the lesson stall.

- The teacher loses steam and the direction of the lesson.

- The teacher talks less resulting in the group talking more – both without purpose.

- The teacher talks in circles, resulting in lack of involvement by the group and lack of ownership of the experience.

- There is a lack of awareness of the presence and movement of the Holy Spirit.

- The teacher's ideas rather than God and His truth become the focus.

- No effort is made to lead learners to open God's Word or meet Him themselves.

- The teacher only shares (1) a testimony about his or her personal encounter with God while preparing the lesson, (2) notes or thoughts from study without an encounter, or (3) thoughts without study or an encounter.

- The lesson makes no sense.

- Fun and work are not balanced, and the experience becomes drudgery and unproductive.

- The end of the lesson is rushed, incomplete, or missing.

- No time is given for thinking, reflection, or silence in response to the lesson or truth.

- The experience is a string of unconnected and fruitless activities rather than a planned encounter producing life change.

- Examination of God's Word takes place without any application to life or any invitation to respond.

- No involvement is sought and no assignments are made.

- No attempt is made to capture or maintain attention of learners.

- The lesson doesn't relate to learners.

- Group time becomes a cognitive dump rather than an attempt to lead learners toward transformation.

- At the lesson's end, disciples have not made spiritual progress.

- Relationships are not strengthened.

- Bible study session remains superficial.

- Guests are not involved.

- No challenge has been extended or plans made for the world to be touched and disciples made.

- The Lord is not honored.

Unfortunately, the list could be longer. An excellent life-impacting second encounter begins with an investment in the first encounter and good lesson planning. The early moments are vital to prepare for, create interest in, and launch the second encounter.

A group leader works toward a revolutionary second encounter moving purposefully into the middle moments, leading learners to know and act on the truth. Neglect is too common here because finishing the second encounter well is hard work, but it is well worth the effort because lives and the world depend on the outcome.

CHAPTER 14

TRANSFORMATIONAL SECOND ENCOUNTER MIDDLE MOMENTS

You have prepared well and spent personal time with God in Bible study. You met Him and were impacted by the encounter. Previous encounters have heightened your expectation of sharing this experience with your group, so you prepared a great lesson plan designed to lead the group to meet God in Bible study.

You showed up early, prayer-walked and prepared the space. You greeted group members and pointed to a poster where you had written an icebreaker question. After a time of announcements, prayer requests, and prayer, you launched the second encounter by reviewing last week's lesson and discussing the icebreaker. You read the Scripture passage. What will happen now?

A PICTURE OF THE SECOND ENCOUNTER

Allow me to share a picture of what could happen in the middle moments of the second encounter. It is not a detailed plan and not intended to represent the plan for every lesson.

Before painting the picture, let me remind you that every

passage, group, and day makes each second encounter experience unique. What do I mean?

When listening to God in the first encounter, how you teach the Exodus passage about the ten plagues on Egypt should be different from how you teach the Acts 2 passage about the day of Pentecost. Also, how you teach a group of teenage girls should vary considerably from how you teach a group of senior adult men. And how you teach on the day after the death of a group member would likely vary from the day after a group ministry project. But at the same time, you may have a standard framework from which you work each week, adjusting each lesson from that framework. See Appendix 1 (first encounter) and Appendix 2 (second encounter) for framework elements.

Here is what I suggest in Appendix 2 to include in middle moments:

- Maintain expectancy and good attitudes.

- Use the Bible: Read and examine Scripture.

- Set Scripture into context.

- Use good teaching methods to address learning styles.

- Make assignments to smaller groups.

- Call for reports of groups.

- Recognize the relevance of the truth for the original audience.

- Allow the Holy Spirit to work.

SAMPLE OPENING AND MIDDLE MOMENT PLAN

Here are some ideas filling in the framework mentioned above for the opening and middle moments of the second encounter.

This is an example of one way to teach this lesson to a coed group of middle-aged adults. This lesson focuses on the Prodigal Son, Elder Son, and the Father in Luke 15:11-32.

OPENING MOMENTS (TWENTY MINUTES):
By the time you get to the middle moments, the following should already be completed:

- When group members entered, you pointed to two questions designed to create interest: (1) Were you the oldest, youngest, or middle child in your family growing up? (2) What difference did birth order make in your family? You gave them an index card to write down responses.

- You started on time with the groups sitting in sub-groups (three to five members and guests).

- A group member shared a couple of announcements.

- Prayer requests were shared and pairs prayed followed by caring contact assignments.

- You then closed the opening moments of the second encounter by reviewing last week's lesson and previewing this week's lesson, emphasizing the importance of what they were about to experience. You led the group in prayer that God would speak to each heart.

MIDDLE MOMENTS (TWENTY-FIVE MINUTES):
Following completion of the opening, you dive into the middle moments:

- The group is still sitting in subgroups when you pose six questions about the lesson. You ask the group to keep them in mind as they listen carefully to God in the time of examination ahead.

- A group member who had agreed last week holds a Bible but tells the parable.

- Share context information: Luke as the author; mixed audience of tax collectors/sinners and Pharisees/scribes; and the main characters in the parable.

- Call on a group member to share some cultural and historical information related to the group about inheritance.

Pass out unique assignments to the three subgroups. The assignments ask questions about the verses, words, and characters. Each assignment concludes with this question: What hope was offered in theses verses to the original audience: (1) tax collectors and sinners, (2) Pharisees and scribes, and (3) Jesus' disciples? Groups have eight minutes to prepare a report.

After subgroup time, you read the Scripture passage and call on the first group to share their questions/responses. Make a few comments and allow others to do the same. Repeat the process for the second and third subgroups (if used).

Do you see each of the middle moment elements from Appendix 2 built into this plan?

- (The fifteen minutes for Closing Moments will be covered in chapters 16-18.)

SECOND ENCOUNTER REMINDERS

While parts of the remainder of this chapter may be common practice for you, these comments will serve as a reminder of what should shape a revolutionary, life-changing, second encounter.

GIVE GOD YOUR BEST

Life-changing Bible study leaders desire more than to do a good job. Like Olympic athletes, they want to give their best. They know that God deserves no less. The people for whom God sent His Son and with whom He has made us shepherd-stewards deserve no less (Heb. 13:20-21). We must be intentional and strategic, and we must not do this work alone, in our own strength.

ALLOW THE SPIRIT TO WORK

You are never teaching alone. This is so reassuring. The Spirit is intimately involved in the lives of believers and in the teaching and learning process. Matt Capps wrote a great blog post entitled, "Ten Principles for Effective Teaching in the Church."[16] In that post, he lists many great applicable Scripture passages:

The Holy Spirit

1. works through the teacher (1 Cor. 12:4-11; 1 Pet. 4:10),

2. illuminates the learner (1 Cor. 2:1-16; Eph. 1:17-19),

3. indwells the learner (John 14:17; Rom. 5:5; 8:9; Eph. 1:13-14),

4. instructs the learner (John 14:26-27; 16:7-15), and

5. draws learners to Himself through teaching (2 Cor. 4:1-6).

The Holy Spirit guides in the preparation process, in our relationships, in teaching and learning, and in applying the Word. The teacher must stay sensitive to the work of the Spirit in his or her personal encounter with God and in serving as guide for learners to do the same. Pray for and leave room for His work in and through you.

---

16   Matt Capps, "Ten Principles for Effective Teaching in the Church," *https://matthewzcapps.com/2008/10/27/ten-principles-for-effective-teaching-in-the-church* (January 18, 2017).

WORK TOWARD LIFE CHANGE

Don't forget that the goal is not merely the act of teaching and communicating or content delivery or increased knowledge. Instead, the goal is to lead learners to encounter God in His Word. This in turn leads them to realize their need to adjust their lives to Him. This encounter is about transformation, becoming more like Jesus. It is growing in the fruit of the Spirit: love, joy, peace, patience, kindness, goodness, faithfulness, gentleness, and self-control (Gal. 5:22-23).

In the Great Commission, Jesus commanded us to make disciples and teach them to obey everything He commanded. Obedience is our goal in teaching – not knowledge. That fact impacts methods, involvement of learners, and expectations.

What does God expect as a result of meeting Him in Bible study? How does He expect you to respond? This requires the teacher to know learners' needs to best lead them to consider the truth of God's Word and put it into practice. The revolutionary teacher works with the Holy Spirit and learners to strive for life change. Nothing less will do.

CAPITALIZE ON THE PHYSICAL ENVIRONMENT

While learning space, equipment, and furnishings do not tend to impact learning as much as relational factors, they are still important. As a reminder, when a space is too warm or too cold, learning is inhibited. Since communication is 93% nonverbal, seating in rows is less effective because communication through gestures, facial expression, and tone may be missed. Rows tend to discourage dialogue.[17]

In addition, since 65% of people are visual learners, it is important to take full advantage of the space to add visual elements to the teaching/learning experience: maps, posters,

---

17   Debenham, *www.bodylanguageexpert.co.uk/communication-what-percentage-body-language.html* (January 11, 2017).

movie clips, and more.[18] Finally, if a space is inaccessible for attenders who have physical challenges, learning is impossible. Choose space wisely and take full advantage of what is available to lead the group to meet God in Bible study.

CAPITALIZE ON THE RELATIONAL ENVIRONMENT

Every individual in the group is unique. Each person has a different personality and set of spiritual gifts, passions, experiences, and abilities. The second encounter varies considerably from one group to the next. It is the teacher's responsibility to make the most of that context. The following principles will help.

GET LEARNERS INVOLVED. Participation is vital in the second encounter for meeting God, teaching effectiveness, and retention. In fact, effective teachers spend time getting to know group members' preferred learning styles and use teaching methods to incorporate those learning styles. Life-changing teachers believe in total period teaching, involving the group from the moment they enter the learning space. Early icebreakers help the attenders relax and make contributions later in the session.

When learners are involved, they tend to feel more satisfaction about the learning experience. When they enjoy themselves, they are more likely to attend regularly and invite friends.

Group members will then remember more of what was taught and apply the truth and lesson to their lives. In other words, involvement in the lesson often results in life adjustments. They are more likely to become disciples who obey.

Ask questions. Break the group into smaller groups. Recognize that learning continues after group time ends. Give assignments between second encounters. Ask review questions to see what was learned and what was applied.

---

18   Vakos, *www.phschool.com/eteach/social_studies/2003_05/essay.html* (January 11, 2017).

Group members have much to contribute. Involve them in the second encounter and watch enjoyment, learning, and application of God's Word increase.

ASSESS LEARNERS' NEEDS. One of the best ways to discover learners' needs is to spend time with them outside of group sessions in their homes, at work or school, in recreational opportunities, at events, and in ministry projects. Spend time listening and get to know them, their hopes and dreams, challenges they face, as well as their spiritual progress. This helps increase your effectiveness as you teach to meet real needs.

In addition, sometimes asking your group to complete a survey can help gather a lot of information quickly. I don't recommend a survey in place of spending time with group members. Instead, I recommend a survey in addition to spending time with them. Also, shorter surveys often produce more results. Here is a sample series of questions that may help you consider their needs as you prepare lessons for life change:

- What do you like most about our group? Why?

- How could we improve our group sessions, organization, and activities?

- What would you be willing to do to make our group stronger?

- Have you ever invited anyone to our group? Who could you invite in the next month?

- How would you rate your spiritual growth on a scale of 1 to 10 with 1 being low? Why would you rate yourself at that level?

- Where do you need help to grow spiritually?

- If you have accepted Jesus as Savior and Lord,

when did you do so? Have you ever told someone about Jesus? Would you be willing to learn how?

- Which two of the nine fruits of the Spirit do you have the greatest difficulty living out: love, joy, peace, patience, kindness, goodness, faithfulness, gentleness, or self-control? Why are they difficult for you?

- Circle what you would be comfortable doing during group time: praying, reading Scripture, and answering questions.

- What life challenges are causing the most stress in your life right now?

- How can I pray for you and your family?

Answers to these or similar questions will help you prepare and teach to meet real life needs. Getting to know group members beyond group time is well worth the time and effort.

INCORPORATE VARIOUS LEARNING STYLES. An effective teacher desires that every attender listen to God to learn and apply the truth every week. To aid that effort, the teacher spends time getting to know each learner individually. And the teacher pays attention to responses during the second encounter.

While learning style assessments may be administered to the group (see Appendix 3), the teacher can learn a great deal by observing each group member during various learning activities. No two learners are alike. Some learners are introverts; others are extroverts. Some are inner thinkers; others are outer thinkers. Some are thinkers; others are feelers. Personality differences also shape interaction and plans.

The worst teaching method is the one used all the time. Even if the usual method addresses preferred learning styles of several group members, routine leads to boredom.

*The best method is the one that addresses the truth
of Scripture in the best possible way with this group
of learners at this point in time.*

If a method used produces no positive results, assess why it failed. Instructions may not be clear. Maybe the method was interrupted. Maybe the method did not connect with learners and their learning styles. If so, be cautious about using that method again. Energy, learning, and life change are measures of a method's effectiveness. If these three things are missing, it is likely time to ditch the method. Follow God's leadership as you prayerfully consider your group.

Life-changing, second encounters require focus on the way group members learn. Knowledge of them and their preferred learning styles help when preparing and delivering appropriate teaching methods. Be prayerful and purposeful in using a variety of teaching methods in your second encounter plan.

SEEK TRANSFORMATION

For too many years, the body of Christ has taken the command to *make disciples* too lightly. How can Bible study groups help the church make disciples?

What would happen if groups began to produce disciples? What would that look like? What would be the impact of groups leading members to seek God's power and leadership in prayer? What would happen if they sought his will and ways through listening to His still, small voice when they opened His Word in personal and corporate Bible study? What would result from Bible study groups leading members to apply God's truth (obey Jesus' commands)? Groups can do so much more.

What adjustments to thinking and practice do group leaders need to make? Out of many potential adjustments, consider these four transformation points as you prepare for and teach the second encounter:

TRANSFORMATION IS ABOUT MORE THAN FORGIVENESS FROM SIN. Christians should not rest on the laurels of a conversion experience. Our Lord expects more. We are to work out our salvation: *So then, my dear friends, just as you have always obeyed, not only in my presence, but now even more in my absence, work out your own salvation with fear and trembling* (Phil. 2:12).

James reminds us that discipling requires faithful action:

> *What good is it, my brothers, if someone says he has faith but does not have works? Can his faith save him? If a brother or sister is without clothes and lacks daily food and one of you says to them, "Go in peace, keep warm, and eat well," but you don't give them what the body needs, what good is it?* (James 2:14-16)

The second encounter is an opportunity to teach obedience to what Jesus commanded. Members come to understand and respond to Jesus' words when they are encouraged to live out the truth:

> *If anyone wants to come with Me, he must deny himself, take up his cross daily, and follow Me.* (Luke 9:23)

TRANSFORMATION RESULTS IN BEING JESUS' APPRENTICES. What if teachers focused on training members to be Jesus' apprentices? What if group members understood they were to be a reflection of Jesus in the world? What if Bible study groups became a source of training and mobilization for carrying out kingdom work in the world? This change begins during the second encounter and is reinforced one-on-one. What if every attender was paired with another for accountability to apply God's truth? What if every disciple then invested in someone beyond the group?

TRANSFORMATION IS MORE THAN EXTERNAL. The second encounter is a great place to learn what a disciple looks and acts like. But it goes deeper than the superficial. It goes beyond actions and focuses on the heart and intent. The second encounter helps attenders transform from an unbeliever, who *does not welcome what comes from God's Spirit,* to a disciple (1 Cor. 2:14). The second encounter can lead group members to recognize and deal with sin while learning to display the fruit of the Spirit (Gal. 5:22).

This time can help the group clean the inside of their cups: *Woe to you, scribes and Pharisees, hypocrites! You clean the outside of the cup and dish, but inside they are full of greed and self-indulgence! Blind Pharisee! First clean the inside of the cup, so the outside of it may also become clean* (Matt. 23:25-26). Together it can hold attenders accountable to *be* and *live* like Jesus.

TRANSFORMATION RECOGNIZES GREAT POWER FOR HUGE TASKS. Don't forget the power that is available through the Spirit. Meeting God in Bible study during the second encounter has potential to mobilize members into big, life-impacting, kingdom actions. What if every member found a way to serve and invested in a lost person to love to Jesus? What if they prayed big prayers and believed God would answer? What if they believed what Paul wrote to the Philippian believers?

> *I am able to do all things through Him who strengthens me. (Phil. 4:13)*

What adjustment do you need to make to be a transformed disciple? These adjustments may also be the first steps needed to lead your group in that direction. What steps can you take to transform your babes in Christ into His disciples? What is the next step your group needs to take to become His apprentices? What sins do your members need to address? What fruit of the Spirit needs to be practiced? Plan and lead intentional steps toward transformation.

BE A PERPETUAL LEARNER

Life-changing group leaders never stop learning. They learn about God, His Word, the biblical context and customs, and biblical languages. They also learn about teaching and are willing to try new things. They attend training and conferences and observe the way others teach. They take advantage of teachable moments in life.

These teachers are not afraid to ask others to observe their teaching and offer suggestions. Why? Because they want to improve. They want to teach as effectively as possible. This requires humility, but the benefits are worth honest feedback. Great second encounters require that teachers never stop learning about God, the Bible, and teaching.

SUMMARY

Focus on God and His Word in these moments. What are some words of wisdom for leading the middle moments of the second encounter? Give God your best effort, as you involve the Spirit in the first and second encounter. Work toward life change and lead group members toward it. Take advantage of the learning environment. Involve learners. Assess learner needs; then customize the teaching plan to individual learners. Be a perpetual learner. Settle for nothing less than transformation: yours and theirs.

CHAPTER 15

SECOND ENCOUNTER MIDDLE MOMENT CHALLENGES

Even in an ideal physical and relational environment, sometimes middle moment challenges exist. How you handle these challenges will either move the group toward or away from the encounter God desires.

Some of these challenges come from the way individuals in your group interact with each other. Some may be quiet while others are too talkative. Some may know and trust one another while others are new and unsure. The second encounter would be perfect if it wasn't for people. But seriously, the best teachers are not only great facilitators of a second encounter with God in His Word, they are also great facilitators of relational environment challenges.

HANDLING RELATIONAL CHALLENGES

Three of the more common relationship challenges are people won't talk, talk too much, and take us on rabbit trails. Handling these in an appropriate way can change the entire group experience.

LACK OF PARTICIPATION

After a few weeks of teaching the oldest men, my father-in-law was ready to throw in the towel. He couldn't get them to talk, so lessons were ending early. After hearing his preparation routine and what he did on Sunday, Larry revealed that he would ask questions but would also give the answer if no one responded. I told him not to answer. Some people are uncomfortable with silence and will eventually answer a question if silence lasts long enough. When he tried it the next week, it worked too well. They began talking, and Larry found it difficult to finish on time.

A couple more methods for getting people to talk are ice-breakers and dividing the group into smaller groups. When you want everyone to talk, get them into pairs. Even groups of three to six individuals will be more likely to converse than if the attenders stay in a group larger than six. Remember, involvement is more likely to produce enjoyment, retention, and life change.

TOO MUCH PARTICIPATION

Without a doubt, the development of a poor teaching plan contributes to talking too much by the teacher and by one or more individuals. Prepare a good plan and manage it well. Some groups do have dominators who talk too much. There are several ways to handle dominators:

1. *REDIRECT.* One way to redirect attention from the dominator is to call on people other than the domi-nator. Also, sitting next to the dominator reduces eye contact and may reduce comments.

2. *GROUP COVENANT.* Set some second encounter rules. Because everyone's contribution is important, ask the group in advance to allow everyone to talk once before speaking a second time.

3. *ONE-ON-ONE.* Talk to the dominator. Affirm their contributions, but ask for their help. Tell them that you are trying to get more people involved and ask them to allow at least three comments by others before talking again.

4. *CONFRONT.* You might need to confront the individual more directly and forcefully. Help the dominator understand the impact his or her behavior has on the group. This is best done privately, but reminders may also be needed during group time.

5. *AFFIRM.* Affirm responses from other people. Doing so can encourage regular contributions from others besides the dominator.

6. *DON'T DO IT.* Avoid being the dominator yourself. If you are talking more than half of the time, you need to develop a better second encounter plan. Back off and facilitate the conversation for others and watch what God does!

RABBIT TRAILS

Some have opinions about everything. Do your best to keep the plan on course, steering away from opinions and back to God's Word. Be quick to reign in any attempt that leads the group astray. A good plan with a tentative time schedule keeps things flowing.

NEW PEOPLE AND GUESTS

The number one fear for many people today is public speaking. In fact, placing someone in the spotlight or forcing them to speak to a group all but ensures that they will not return. In light of that, remember these four don'ts:

DON'T ASK THEM TO INTRODUCE THEMSELVES. When guests visit or new persons join the group, the greeter should get to know them and introduce them to the group. This requires the greeter to spend some one-on-one time with the guest. Make sure to pronounce the name correctly and provide name tags for everyone. Get good contact information so follow up contacts can be made. A comfortable introduction eases second encounter fears.

DON'T ASK THEM TO READ ALOUD. Keep in mind that 50% of Americans struggle with reading skills.[19] A small percentage cannot read. Many cannot read well, and some just do not like to read aloud (reading aloud is public speaking). Avoid asking guests or new people to read aloud unless you have asked them privately about their willingness to do so. Embarrassment will tend to end second encounter openness to God.

DON'T ASK THEM TO PRAY. For some, private prayer is fine, but praying in front of the group is not. Some have never been taught how to pray and would be too insecure to do so aloud. Others just fear the public speaking side of prayer. Ask them privately about their willingness to pray. If they volunteer to pray, don't stop them.

DON'T ASK THEM TO ANSWER QUESTIONS. Calling on an individual to answer a question in front of the group is asking them to speak publicly. If they volunteer an answer when a question is asked to the group, let them answer. They are obviously comfortable doing so. But don't call on them individually unless you already know they are comfortable with it.

One misstep in any of these public speaking traps can impact the second encounter. Not dealing with those who are too quiet,

---

19   Mark Snowden, "The Unreached Half: Wrenching Statistics on Literacy in America," Truthsticks, *https://truthsticks.wordpress.com/2015/02/01/the-unreached-half-wrenching-statistics-on-literacy-in-america* (January 18, 2017).

are too talkative, or create rabbit trails has great potential for taking the focus away from God, His Word, and His plan for the lives of those in the group. Handle these challenges prayerfully and purposefully so that lives can be changed.

PART FIVE

SECOND ENCOUNTER CLOSING MOMENTS

BATTLES OF BRANDYWINE AND GERMANTOWN

Near the end of August 1777, British General Howe brought his army south by sea to threaten Philadelphia. On September 10, they attacked American troops, blocking the way at Brandywine. In a day-long battle, the British had the upper hand over colonial forces. The American army withdrew to fight another day.

With the loss of Philadelphia, the Continental Congress evacuated to New Jersey before finally settling in Annapolis. After Howe's occupation of Philadelphia, Washington launched a four-pronged attack on British troops at Germantown on October 4. Unfortunately, the morning was foggy and Continental Army coordination broke down. Consequently, the attack failed and American troops were forced to retreat.[20]

---

20   History.com Staff, "The Battle of Germantown," *History.com,* 2009, *www.history.com/topics/american-revolution/battle-of-germantown,* (January 11, 2017).

CHAPTER 16

NEGLECT OF SECOND ENCOUNTER CLOSING MOMENTS

CRUCIAL CLOSING MOMENTS

When the second encounter doesn't go the way we planned, we just regroup and keep moving forward. We must trust the Spirit to use the experience; we can count on God having a message for us when we open His Word. The message and encounter are personal and life-changing. They are invitations to a real and personal relationship with a mighty God – invitations to trust Him, follow Him, and obey Him.

Every time we open God's Word, whether privately or as a group, we discover an opportunity to respond to God's individual invitation. Every Bible study session should lead to a personal response. In fact, the invitation during the closing moments should be prayed for, planned, and never rushed.

SOURCES OF NEGLECT

Closing moments are too important to be neglected. But like the American troops forced to retreat in the fog, lack of coordination can cause defeat or failure. Complication, interruption, and confusion of closing moments should be anticipated and group time rerouted when possible. Several factors contribute to neglecting the closing moments.

A FIZZLING FINISH

Sometimes parts of the study time last longer than planned, and no time remains for the invitation. Too many lessons start well and then fizzle. Time runs out just as individuals are recognizing their need to adjust their lives to the truth of God's Word. Or the moments are wasted. Interruptions occur. The stirring of the Spirit is quenched. Instead of sizzle, the lesson simply ends.

POOR PLANNING

Why did this happen? Was it poor planning? Did the teacher run out of time during the first encounter to plan for this part of the second encounter? Does the teacher not know how to handle these moments?

When the teacher has not planned for closing moments filled with excitement and purpose, the lesson will cruise off course. The plane will never land. Poor planning will result in a poorly balanced understanding of how much time each part of the lesson will take. A domino effect will take over, usually impacting the end of the lesson more than any other.

POOR TIME MANAGEMENT

Did the teacher fail to plan enough time for discussion? Or did the teacher hesitate to rein in the rabbit trails? Or were too many methods crammed into the middle moments, filling time needed for closing moments?

Good time management begins with knowing how much time is available and how much time each section of the lesson should take. There should be major markers or transitions during the group time. Let's look at an example of a one-hour schedule:

- start time/get attention (9:00 a.m.)
- group business: announcements/prayer (9:01-9:10 a.m.)
- opening moments (9:10-9:20 a.m.)
- middle moments (9:20-9:45 a.m.)
- closing moments (9:45-9:59 a.m.)
- end time (10:00 a.m.)

Without a plan, you will not start on time, stay on time, or end on time. Notice each section has a start and end time, meaning each segment has a time allowance. If group business lasts longer than the allotted time, it impacts everything that follows. If you cram too much in the opening or middle moments, the closing moments will suffer.

Within each section, the teacher must plan all activities to fit into the allotted time. If you add a great but lengthy method to the opening moments, you must make adjustments elsewhere in the schedule. You may need to start early, maybe even before the Bible study time is scheduled to begin, reduce the number of announcements, or skip other normal opening moment actions.

START ON TIME

Perhaps neglect of closing moments started at the beginning. Did the group fail to start on time? If you wait to start until everyone shows up, you are simply training the group to show up late. Instead, explain when you will start the group. Help the group understand why it is important. Then implement the plan. Remind them every week for a month. You might make a few calls or send email reminders. If some are chronic latecomers, you might even consider moving group business to the end. Start the lesson first. Some will not want to miss life-changing time with God in His Word.

GROUP BUSINESS

If the group started on time, did announcements and prayer take too much time? Neglect of opening moments can occur through lengthy group business when there is no targeted end time and no one in charge. Assign group business to a member and explain that their job is to start and end business on time. If something special comes up, find a creative way to shorten everything else – perhaps print the announcements and give everyone a copy or send them in an email.

AMOUNT OF MATERIAL

Could the problem have been that the teacher simply planned too much material? Was there an attempt to focus on too many verses and too much background and history to handle these closing moments well? Middle moments should set up the closing moments, but covering too much material will often produce confusion over the point.

Sometimes less is more. Teachers often try to communicate three or four points in each lesson, and at the end of the hour, few can remember even one of the points. What if one truth is communicated and reinforced with everything studied and every method used? What if at the end of the middle moments, the group heard God's message to them and were ready in the closing moments to respond to Him?

It is the teacher's job to decide which methods are crucial for communicating the truth and preparing the group for needed changes. And if a method takes too much time, the teacher must choose what to cut to ensure that the closing moments are not neglected.

For the life-changing teacher, closing moments are a priority. Since the purpose is for group members to encounter God in His Word and be changed, the close of the lesson is vital. What happens in those closing moments is the point of the hour. Other parts of the group time can be cut, but not the closing.

INTERRUPTIONS

Naturally some interruptions are unavoidable. The smoke alarm goes off. A church-wide fellowship is planned after worship and chairs from your space are needed before the group normally ends. A staff member arrives to share about a group member in an accident. Interruptions can impact the closing moments unless adjustments are made.

The easiest interruptions to accommodate are the ones known early. If you find out about the chairs or announcement before the group session, adjust your plans for the day. Allow for lost time in advance. Decide what to cut to avoid neglecting the closing moments. Or if necessary, make alternative plans for delivering the closing moment experience at another time, another place, or the following week.

But when there is a history of interruptions, the source may need to be addressed. You may need to talk to the grandmother who comes by to say hello to her grandchild. When several from other group leaders enter the room for paper and Bibles, you may need to ask for items stored in your room to be moved. Try to anticipate all foreseeable interruptions so the closing time is not interrupted or cut short.

RESPONSE CHALLENGE

Don't rush through the Bible study session and forget to give the "invitation." After helping the group understand the truth of God's Word, give them a chance to think about, plan, and commit to live out that truth. Ask them prayerfully to reflect on what God wants them to do.

Check on the commitments they make this week at the start of the next week's Bible study session. Teach them to do more than just know God's Word; teach them to obey what Jesus commanded. Each action takes time. Plan for them. Allow nothing to get in the way. Plan for life change.

CHAPTER 17

APPLICATION STEPS IN THE CLOSING MOMENTS

You had a great time in the first encounter, meeting God in your personal Bible study and lesson preparation. During the week, God led you to make life adjustments. Early, He had already illustrated the lesson truth a couple of times. And He gave you an understanding of the point He wanted the group to understand during the second encounter. You put together a lesson plan to accomplish what He revealed to you.

You arrived early for the Bible study group, prepared and prayer-walked the space, and greeted group members as they arrived. You gave out a printed question to answer before group started. After a meal or fellowship time, a member called the group to start on time. The group gathered in subgroups to make plans to contact absentees and friends. After a couple of announcements, subgroups closed with prayer requests and prayer.

At that point, you stepped forward. You briefly reviewed last week's lesson and asked for testimonies about living out the truth of last week. Then you asked for responses to the printed question they received. The questions and their responses give a little preview to the direction the lesson is going. You shared your excitement about what God did in your life during the week and how important today's encounter with God is.

You left them seated in subgroups and gave each group an assignment with questions about the day's passage. After allowing time to complete the assignment (and listen to God in Bible study), you began going through the lesson and calling for subgroup reports. In this second encounter, the entire group recognized the relevance of truth for the original audience.

Now, with fifteen minutes remaining, you move into the closing moments. There are several actions you will want to accomplish before time runs out:

- summarize and review

- apply

- invite and identify

- commit and pray

- preview and assign

- close in prayer

- end on time

Each of these actions is important. None of them should be forgotten or skipped. They are connected and usually flow together to form the "invitation."

SUMMARIZE AND REVIEW

Today's attention spans are short, so review helps retention and attention. Quickly summarize the lesson. Review key truths or the point of the lesson in historical and today's context. What was God saying then and what is He saying now? Make sure they got it. Some questions here might include:

- What point was the author making to the original hearers?

- Why was this message important back then?

- How is this lesson relevant to people today?

- What is the point that God wants us to realize today?

APPLY

Along with understanding the truth in context, group members need to be led to apply the truth to their lives. They need to be encouraged to evaluate their lives by the truth. There is no single set way to handle applying the truth to their lives.

Some people are external thinkers who prefer to process material out loud. Others are internal thinkers who prefer to do this process privately and internally. So, it is appropriate to handle this in a variety of ways. Since external thinkers can often reach a conclusion more quickly than the second group, this time should not be rushed for the benefit of the internal thinkers who need a bit longer.

Personal application can take the form of a series of questions to the group. It can be a blank index card for response on one or both sides. It can simply be reflection. This can be handled in pairs, in a smaller group (up to six), or as a total group. But application needs to begin during group time.

Make sure they got it. Some questions here might include:

- What did God say to you in today's lesson?

- How does today's truth apply to your life? family? work?

- In what ways did God reveal the need to adjust your life during today's second encounter?

INVITE AND IDENTIFY

When we open God's Word, He has a message for us. The message and encounter are personal and life-changing. They are invitations to a real and personal relationship with God. They are invitations to trust Him, follow Him, and obey Him.

Every Bible study session should lead to a personal response to that invitation. Often the teaching content dominates the time, and no time is given to the invitation (response). This cheats participants from an opportunity to commit to obedience.

Jesus expects us to teach not for head knowledge but for obedience – for life change. To teach content and not give an opportunity to respond in obedience is short-circuiting Jesus' command. That means we must do more than talk. Thoughtful, prayerful response is needed. Time spent carefully planning for the invitation is an essential part of your preparation for the second encounter.

During the identify phase of the invitation, help the group consider possible outcomes. Help them recognize the personal nature of the invitation and identify the response God desires. This may take coaching initially. Some truth during second encounters may not appear to apply, meaning there is no need for a response. But when we meet God in Bible study, there is always a need for a response.

Make sure they understand the personal nature of His invitation. Some questions here might include:

- What adjustments does God desire in your relationship, attitudes, habits, and practices?

- As a result of this study, what changes does God desire in your life?

- What change is needed to bring your life in line with what God said when you met Him in Bible study?

- What do you need to do to be obedient to God's message to you?

COMMITMENT CARDS

The commitment card is one tool to use for group members to express their commitment. Every lesson should lead group members to meet God in Bible study. They should listen to what God says and respond to Him in commitment. Help participants apply the truth of God's Word to their daily lives. An invitation to respond to God should be extended. Most literature offers good suggestions for leading attenders to do this. Unfortunately, I find many teachers shortchange this process. They want to share so much Bible content that they don't allow attenders time to consider what God is saying to them or how they should respond.

Increasing the spiritual maturity of group members means that we need to help them make commitments.

Every time group members open God's Word, He expects a response. How can we help them take the next step?

Commitment cards could be a part of the answer. What if group members were asked to complete a card sharing a commitment they made in response to God in His Word? Giving the card to an attender is an automatic invitation, and their process of writing on it serves as an identification of what they need to do as a commitment. Cards probably shouldn't be used every week, but when used, they can produce great results. An ideal commitment card should be specifically designed based upon the response(s) to that lesson or series of lessons. Think about how you can use cards to increase obedience in the second encounter.

COMMIT AND PRAY

Application of God's Word is not enough. Neither is helping the group understand that God expects a response. Even identifying an expected response falls short.

Commitment is necessary. Agreeing with God is always a minimal response. He is always right, but obedience is what He desires, not just agreement. Commitment is a step toward obedience. It is choosing to obey and telling God how you will do it. It is a personal resolve to act.

For group members, this is a critical step. It is possible that some may still be disagreeing that God is right. The course of action that God desires may be distasteful or difficult, but facing God in His Word, requires response. Disagreement is basically delaying the inevitable.

Commitment and obedience are what He desires. Commitment is often a matter of prayer, so lead them to tell God what they will do because of this encounter. Keep in mind that while this can be done privately or publicly; it is first and foremost a response to God.

This response can be written or verbal. The advantage of sharing your commitment with someone is the encouragement and support that may be received. While some may fear the risk of exposure, trust is built over time when safety in sharing has been practiced. One tool that may help is a journal of response.

JOURNALS AND PEOPLE

How does a teacher lead his or her attenders to obey God's commands? While adults can take knowledge and convert it into action without encouragement and positive accountability, many adults merely learn history lessons, factual content, or moral lessons without changing their thoughts or actions. In other words, many adults miss the step of listening, which is necessary before obedience. After all, how can we obey if we don't listen?

But some do listen to God's still, small voice in Bible study, whether in a Bible study group, worship, or personal quiet time. And some make commitments in those times of Bible study. In my experience, however, the problem is that promises are made to God but not kept. If during Bible study, worship, or private devotions, we tell God we are going to do something and we do not do what we said, we make ourselves liars.

How can we help ourselves as teachers as well as help group members keep commitments? We need to ask ourselves this question: *What did I do because of what God said?* Now, that is a strange question to ask during an encounter with God in Bible study. In fact, it cannot be answered immediately since we have not yet had time to obey.

How can we hold ourselves and attenders accountable to keep our promises to God? I can think of two helpful methods:

(1) *JOURNALS.* Use a spiritual journal by writing the date and Scripture passage and answer the four sets of questions (see first encounter steps from Appendix 4). Then check back on how you and group members are doing in obedience every few days.

(2) *PEOPLE.* Ask other believers to check on and encourage your commitments and obedience. Talk and pray together.

One final reminder: Don't forget to remind the group that you will be asking for testimonies about living out the truth during the week ahead. If they are journaling, remind them that they can share entries. This can be in pairs, small groups, or with the whole group. And don't forget to ask for these the following week.

PREVIEW AND ASSIGN
Time is always precious and in short supply, but giving a minute

or two about next week's lesson and why it is important encourages return. It builds an understanding of why regularity is beneficial. It is a good time to remind them to read the passage, to give them questions to answer, or even to make assignments. Obviously, that means you need to spend a few minutes during your first encounter preparation previewing the Scripture for the next second encounter.

THANK GUESTS

Express appreciation to guests for their participation in the group. Call them by name. Invite them back. If you are meeting in the church building, make sure someone guides them to their children, restrooms, and to worship. And don't forget to contact them within seventy-two hours. During the call, thank them again. Ask if they have any questions. Ask how you can pray for them. Then pray together. This can be done by phone but in person is best.

CLOSE IN PRAYER

Ideally this prayer should reflect what God has said that day and responses shared by group members. The prayer may also seek blessing and preparation for worship ahead, if it is to follow.

END ON TIME

Some teachers end late every week. They want to blame the Spirit, but the same Spirit was involved in the first encounter when they put together the plan for the second encounter. When group time extends beyond the allotted time every week, the blame goes to the planner.

Resolve to end on time and assess every session. Ending on time can also give group members time to reflect further upon what God wants them to do. Give your group time to transition and prepare for worship, if it follows. And help those teachers who are caring for the children of your group members. Starting on time and ending on time is possible when you have planned well for the second encounter.

CHAPTER 18

CHANGE PRACTICES IN THE CLOSING MOMENTS

What if a method existed that was more likely to produce change in the lives of group members? Would you be willing to lead your group through that method? What if the method had three simple steps? Does that make it sound more appealing?

THREE SIMPLE CHANGE STEPS

Demonstrate it. Train them. Reward them. These three steps work. They can help you lead group members to make needed change in their lives.

Determine the change needed in the lives of your attenders. Prayerfully take a few minutes to list possibilities. Then prioritize them, which is most important or which should be done first? Which is second?

After you have identified your priorities, take the following steps:

(1) Demonstrate: You have led the group to encounter God in Bible study, and they understand how the truth applies to life today. Now, how can you help them see the change needed? How can you help them have confidence to make the change? Is it possible that you could model the change in a way that would be understood and motivating? How could you demonstrate it for leaders or members? How can you model it so group members will be prepared to take steps toward obedience?

Example: The passage was John 1:43-51 about Philip leading Nathanael to Jesus. The group recognized the importance of relationships and family. Many identified family members and friends who needed Jesus. As the teacher, demonstrate a simple way for them to share Jesus. Then ask someone else to model it.

(2) Train: How can you train them to understand? How can you foster confidence? How can you teach the change using a variety of methods and in different venues so that it is reinforced and understood? How can you catch their attention through training them so they put it into practice?

Example: With the same example of sharing Jesus, place the group in pairs and lead them to practice sharing the gospel. Practice for ten minutes each week for a month. Ask them to share the gospel with someone during the week as practice. Then send them out to do it.

(3) Reward: How can you affirm early adopters? How can you reward those who implement the change successfully? How can you bring attention to progress in front of the group? How can you reward progress privately?

Example: With sharing Jesus, you could give a book to the first person who told about sharing Jesus with a friend or family member. The group could clap for them. The point is to affirm or recognize those who changed or took steps to live out the truth of God's Word.

Demonstrate it. Train them. Reward them. Simple and yet

powerful. Identify needs and prioritize. These steps will grow out of some lessons naturally, but most will be aided by thinking through these steps. The more we strive to help the group see the change they need to make, the more likely they are to take steps in that direction. Make plans to model, teach, and reward the change that is needed.

FIVE CLOSING PRACTICES

John Ortberg, senior pastor of Menlo Park Presbyterian, identified five practices that transform and energize groups that should be considered: Confession, application, accountability, guidance, and encouragement.[21]

The combination he shares can be life changing during the second encounter, especially when practiced in the closing moments.

CONFESSION

Confession includes honesty with each other *and* with God. Ortberg defined confession this way: "Appropriate disclosure of my brokenness, temptations, sin, and victories for the purpose of healing, forgiveness, and spiritual growth."[22]

The word *appropriate* is one that I had not considered. Groups should avoid inappropriate confession – when the motivation is wrong. Appropriate disclosure realizes the need for growth, change, and help.

The way the group responds to disclosure can impede future confession and life change, but without confession, help is difficult to seek or receive. And change is less likely without support. Trust is essential.

---

21   John Ortberg, "No More Mr. Nice Group," July 4, 2007, *Christian Bible Studies*, *www.christianitytoday.com/biblestudies/articles/spiritualformation/070704. html* (January 18, 2017).

22   Ortberg, "No More Mr. Nice Group."

APPLICATION

Application also relates to honesty – honesty about ourselves and the realization that we have not arrived. We are not finished growing; we have not reached the goal of being like Jesus. We are not perfect. Honesty is a realization among group members of the need to understand the truth of God's Word, be convicted by the truth, determine to apply it, and help one another live it. Ortberg reminds us that small groups are "schools of life."[23] Groups are less about theory and more about practice. They are not simply groups that meet once a week, because encouragement comes as they practice and walk together.

ACCOUNTABILITY

Groups have opportunity and permission to check on each other's progress toward commitments. This is vital. Accountability deals with honesty about our intentions and depends on mutual, open relationships. If we are serious about life change, we need each other, because we are more likely to accomplish our commitments together than alone.

GUIDANCE

Members who have already been where the rest of the group is going can help others navigate the journey. They can share experiences and coach others to move forward. Appropriate guidance denotes leadership, but in the case of a group, there is an openness to leadership from each other and not just from the teacher.

ENCOURAGEMENT

A Bible study group is a body of cheerleaders who care about each other. They want everyone in the group to succeed and grow. They love everyone and want the best for each member.

---

23   Ortberg, "No More Mr. Nice Group."

They pat others on the back; they affirm; they comfort others during difficulty but challenge them to continue forward.

How is your group doing? Which practices are strong? On which of the practices does the group need to work? On which of these five practices do you need to work as you lead the group during second encounter closing moments? Great leaders help their groups excel in all five practices: confession, application, accountability, guidance, and encouragement.

CHAPTER 19

THE THIRD ENCOUNTER

The second encounter is not over just because the group time ends. God desires a relationship with each person 168 hours of every week, not just when gathering for Bible study and worship. Teachers have an opportunity to lead group members to continue the encounter and strengthen that relationship. This is the third encounter. What can you do to lead them to act more like Jesus? How can you move them from members, to ministers, to missionaries, to leaders? How can you lead them from babes in Christ to fully devoted followers to disciple-makers?

DEPEND ON GOD

God is the reason we gather as a group. He is the reason we have something to study together and to apply to our lives. Depend on Him and spend time in His Word and in prayer. Seek Him and seek the power of His Spirit in your life as a Christ follower and as you prepare to lead others to study His Word. Trust Him to lead as you disciple the sheep He has placed in your care. Pray for His guidance and help.

Believe that the same God who met and changed you through the first encounter wants to do so through the second and third encounters. And He wants the fruit of that encounter to produce obedience, life-change, and world impact. Pray for the third encounter to continue daily and for group members to take steps of change and obedience. Pray for huge, world-impacting results!

STAY IN TOUCH

Use every means at your disposal to continue the encounter beyond group time: face-to-face contact, phone, email, text, and social media. Help members prepare for the next week as well as live out the truth from the previous week. Make assignments and give them questions about next week's lesson to answer when they read the passage this week. Encourage them to use the Bible study helps provided by the church.

Challenge members to apply the truth of this week's lesson and let them know you will be asking for testimonies next week; then do it! Remind them about commitments and teach them about a daily quiet time and spiritual disciplines. Help them grow in their relationship with God, each other, and the world.

ACCOUNTABILITY BEYOND GROUP TIME

What if, through prayer, your group became willing to do whatever it took to become better disciples of Jesus? How might you, as a group, do this? One discipling method that could be life-changing is to establish accountability partners. What would they do? How could it work? Consider the following ways for accountability to work beyond the walls of the space:

- form groups of two but no more than four (of the same gender)

- meet for a few minutes together every other week (during or between group time)
- share prayer requests together (writing them)
- pray together (when together or by phone)
- ask about application of last week's lesson
- ask about practicing spiritual disciplines
- encourage one another

What would happen if your group moved in this direction? What might God do in your midst? What would happen to relationships and to the spiritual maturity of the group? How might that attract others to the group? How could you integrate new people into the system? Could a pair of accountability partners accept one more person? Could a pair of accountability partners split up to take two new people? Disciples make disciples in the third encounter.

BE AN EXAMPLE

In my experience, only a small percentage of adults maintain a high level of spiritual discipline on their own. And the number of adults who drop out of church and yet are highly disciplined would be near zero. We need an ongoing third encounter connection with Christ and His body.

> *If anyone does not remain in Me, he is thrown aside like a branch and he withers. They gather them, throw them into the fire, and they are burned. If you remain in Me and My words remain in you, ask whatever you want and it will be done for you.*
> (John 15:6-7)

When individuals remove themselves from the body of Christ, they risk having their fire go out. Bible study groups serve a vital role in assimilating and in developing discipline in disciples. The group often serves as a more personal expression of the body of Christ than large-group worship.

Groups are often confused about this role. It amazes me how many teachers and groups talk about wanting to go deeper in God's Word while at the same avoiding any discussion about accountability. They often argue that accountability is best left between the individual and God. When they do this, they fail to see the benefit of the group as an encourager, challenger, and supporter of spiritual growth.

What would some accountability actions during the second and third encounters look like?

GROUP TIME DISCIPLING SUPPORT: Direct the group to pair off each week (same pair when possible) to ask each other: (a) how they are doing spiritually, (b) how they are growing, (c) how they are struggling, and (d) how they need prayer. Pray for one another at this time and throughout the week.

ENCOURAGEMENT: Write the questions from above on cards and give them to attenders to complete and return. These could be reviewed by a group encourager who would respond during the week.

APPLICATION FOLLOW-UP: At the beginning of every session, ask what success attenders had applying last week's truth. Expect responses.

MEMBER CARE LEADERS: Enlist member care leaders to guide group members to be concerned about the spiritual progress of group members.

ACCOUNTABILITY GROUPS: Organize the group by gender to hold one another accountable.

AWAY-FROM-GROUP TIME PRAYER PARTNERS: Group prayer partners meet twice a month in person or by phone to pray and check on personal practices of Bible study, prayer, obedience, and sharing Jesus.

Which of these could be accomplished in a group that remains open to new members? All of them could with intentional leadership and desire. A group that took encouragement, discipling, and accountability seriously would become attractive to others. Current participants would realize they are making spiritual progress and would be excited to tell others about the group. Current participants would be more likely to live lives that reflect our Lord and Savior and would be more attractive to the world.

Pray, brainstorm, and choose discipling actions that fit your group. Patiently reinforce and encourage. Keep your eyes open and check on progress. Look for opportunities to affirm growth and make disciples. Keep in mind that your efforts can go beyond the time that the group is together.

DISCIPLING SCORECARD

How can you continue the second encounter to help group members move from listeners to believers, from believers to followers, from followers to disciples, and from disciples to disciplers? A new scorecard may help.

There are many purposes for scorecards, but they can be used to measure current reality. They can be helpful for reporting essential statistics, useful in shifting focus to areas needing attention and improvement, and add value and affirmation to actions that produce success.

What gets measured gets done. For years, some churches used a scorecard – a six-point record system. Attenders reported contacts, worship attendance, Bibles brought, Bibles read daily, lessons studied, and giving. These were measures of discipling.

Was self-reporting through this scorecard accurate? Probably not. But through the scorecard, discipling received more attention and likely more practice. Today in most churches, the primary statistics on the scorecard are enrollment and attendance. And few churches use either statistic to encourage disciple growth.

It is time for the development of a new Bible study group scorecard. In most cases, the second encounter will spawn many of the ideas and commitments by individuals and the group. For any scorecard to be effective, some practices are needed: planning, communicating/training, tracking/reporting, challenging, and rewarding must be put into place.

PLANNING

Gather a leadership team from your group or Bible study ministry to consider what to include on your discipling scorecard. Decide on critical actions that can be measured to reinforce or encourage growth as disciples. This can impact your prayer and planning during the second encounter.

COMMUNICATING/TRAINING

Like all new systems, training and communication are needed before and after implementation. Consider why it is important: How will it help? What do group members need to do and know? Then enlist and train an individual who will be thoroughly versed in, lead, and cheer for the measures and system. Reminders help group members build a plan for their own discipleship. Some communication and training will naturally take place during the second encounter, but some will take place during the third encounter – between group meeting times.

TRACKING/REPORTING

A discipling scorecard is useless unless behavior can be measured, tracked, and reported. Items on the scorecard that cannot be quantified are difficult to encourage. There are many systems of reporting: written, verbal, perception, practice, self-reporting, assessments, surveys, or questionnaires. The planning team should establish a reporting system and take the system on a trial run in advance of rolling it out. Tracking and reporting can be reinforced through testimonies and follow up on what group members did in living out the previous lesson.

CHALLENGING

Key leaders share the importance of measuring discipling actions. Ideally these key leaders also share personal illustrations of their practices in support of the new scorecard. Challenges include goals, deadlines, and rewards. Testimonies, verbal challenges, and goals bring encouragement and motivation to start and continue efforts.

REWARDING

We should reward group members when they report actions they took in response to the challenge. Two rewards should not be forgotten: God's blessings and self-satisfaction. In addition, other rewards can be big or small, but the action of rewarding (even verbal recognition) those who took some discipling steps is vital to the effort.

POTENTIAL MEASUREMENTS

What are some of the discipling actions that could be encouraged, measured, and reported? Choose some of the following practices that might help your group take their next steps of discipling? Circle the ones that resonate:

- Stay involved in a Bible study group

- Spend time with Christ through Bible reading and prayer
- Contact those with needs
- Reach out to contacts
- Invite new group members
- Serve in Bible study and church
- Serve in the community and world
- Enlist new leaders
- Start new groups
- Train leaders
- Share testimonies
- Invite guests to group sessions, socials, projects, and meals
- Report disciples making spiritual progress (from babe to teen to adult)
- Encourage giving and tithing
- Involve more individuals

We can then measure the following to give an indication of whether these practices are making a difference:

- The number of persons in attendance during the last month
- The number of groups adopting an ongoing ministry in the community/world
- The number of conversations members initiated with pre-Christian people

What else would you add to this list? Make your scorecard

simple and don't try to measure too many things or you will create confusion. Focus your scorecard and plan. Communicate and train. Track and report. Challenge. Reward. Don't just have Bible study – make disciples.

EXPECT FRUIT

Let me ask three sets of questions. First, what is the fruit of an orange tree? I have heard the answers of "an orange" and "seeds." Some might also say that the tree produces leaves, shade, and a little windbreak. These would be fruit of sorts. And each of those answers are at least partially correct.

FRUIT OF AN ORANGE TREE

An orange tree does not produce fruit so you and I can enjoy eating an orange. An orange tree produces oranges so it can produce seeds that will grow into more orange trees. It produces oranges to continue the species. God made it that way. The real fruit of an orange tree is an orange tree.

FRUIT OF A DISCIPLE

What is the fruit of a disciple? Could the fruit be a discipled mind, heart, will, or life? Some would argue the fruit of a disciple is glorifying God. That response is hard to argue against.

Could the fruit of a disciple be actions that make him or her look more like Jesus? Both responses head in the right direction. They partially answer the "why" question, but there is more.

Why did Jesus train twelve disciples? Was it to be with Him? Yes, but there was more. Was it to do good in the world? Yes, but there was more. Jesus trained disciples to make disciples of the whole world. Disciples of Jesus understand that the fruit of a disciple is more disciples.

FRUIT OF A BIBLE STUDY GROUP

What is the fruit of a Bible study group? More Bible knowledge is a small part of it. Some say fellowship and assimilation are the fruit, but application of the Word must be part of it.

Certainly, some of the fruit involves changed lives, touching individuals in the community, and fellowship around the Word. Group members telling others about Jesus flows naturally as fruit of a group. We cannot forget to mention worship, encouragement, and accountability. Leading participants to serve God must be part of the fruit. Stronger families and relationships are fruit as well.

But what is the purpose of a group producing fruit? All the previous characteristics are ways to prepare the group to start another group. The fruit of a group is to produce another group that will also produce fruit, much fruit. Jesus told his disciples, *I am the true vine, and My Father is the vineyard keeper. Every branch in Me that does not produce fruit He removes, and He prunes every branch that produces fruit so that it will produce more fruit* (John 15:1-2). Like the orange tree, the group multiplies and continues the species.

HOW THIRD ENCOUNTERS PRODUCE FRUIT

Without more sheep pens, we cannot disciple and care for more sheep. Without new wineskins, we tend to lose new wine. If groups stop multiplying, fewer disciples will emerge – not more.

When a fruit tree stops producing fruit, its usefulness ends. Rededicate your group this year to being fruitful and remember that disciples and group multiplication flow naturally out of the second and third encounters, out of meeting God in Bible study and obeying Him. Pray. Apprentice a new leader and prepare the group to launch another group. What fruit are you preparing your members and group to produce?

FINAL THOUGHTS

Much is at stake. Groups have trained millions of Christians over the years. But too many groups have experienced too little growth in numbers or maturity. Many churches and denominations are in decline and too many disciples look too much like the world, which weakens the impact upon the communities and the world. There is a huge need for passionate disciples who regularly meet God in Bible study and respond in obedience.

To achieve these results, business as usual in our groups will not work. Change is needed. The time is now. Change starts with the teacher spending time with God in Bible study during the first encounter. Out of a life-changing encounter, the teacher can then guide the group on a journey to experience a similar encounter. Then the third encounter of obedience continues throughout the week.

Some shifts in the Bible study experience must take place for that to occur. The teacher must move from being a content expert to becoming a facilitator of the encounter. Group members must become more involved in the encounter. No one can meet God for them. No one can respond to God in their place. No one can walk in obedience for them.

Bible study experiences with an expectancy of meeting God and a willingness to obey teach more than a lesson. They teach the importance of a relationship with God. They teach the importance of a daily quiet time of Bible study and prayer. They teach the need to live lives of obedience. One of the greatest lessons being taught is simply how to listen and respond to God's still, small voice today.

Armed with these kinds of experiences from the second encounter, an army of disciples will go forth into a world that is waiting to hear that Jesus is real and makes a difference. When the world sees changed lives, they will be attracted to a lifestyle different from their own. The door will open wide to share Jesus. With His help, we can make that kind of difference in this generation!

To start your group toward life changes, consider these questions: What do you need to adjust to meet God in Bible study? What do you need to adjust to lead your group to meet Him? Change is not easy, but it is important. Who can provide encouragement as you take needed steps? Where will you start? When will you start? Yesterday is gone, but today is waiting. God and His people deserve your best. He will help. Ask Him right now!

APPENDIX I

FIRST ENCOUNTER

PREPARATION OUTLINE

If your group meets on a day other than Sunday, adjust the preparation outline to fit your schedule. Times are suggested minimums.

SUNDAY (30 MINUTES)
Examine your example (p. 17)
Meet God in your daily quiet time (p. 19)
Read Scripture several times; listen (p. 33)

MONDAY-WEDNESDAY (30 MINUTES EACH DAY)
Examine your example (p. 17)
Meet God in your daily quiet time (p. 19)
Read Scripture several times; listen (p. 33)
Keep your eyes open for life illustrations (p. 41)
Examine the passage and historical context (pp. 22, 33)
Listen for God's message/truth to you (p. 22)
Commit to respond/obey (p. 24)

THURSDAY-FRIDAY (30 MINUTES EACH DAY)

Examine your example (p. 17)

Meet God in your daily quiet time (p. 19)

Read Scripture several times; listen (p. 33)

Keep your eyes open for life illustrations (p. 41)

Apply Scripture to today's context (pp. 22, 33)

Seek specific applications of the truth to group members (p. 34)

Determine adjustments God desires in the lives of group members (p. 35)

SATURDAY (30-60 MINUTES)

Examine your example (p. 17)

Meet God in your daily quiet time (p. 19)

Read Scripture several times; listen (p. 33)

Keep your eyes open for life illustrations (p. 41)

Develop several critical questions (p. 34)

Choose methods that best communicate the truth (p. 34)

Decide on how to create interest and a suitable icebreaker (pp. 47, 93)

Put together a written, second encounter plan (p. 34)

Gather needed resources (p. 54)

Preview next week's Scripture for importance/assignments (pp. 52, 155)

Rest well (p. 33)

SUNDAY

Examine your example (p. 17)

Meet God in your daily quiet time (p. 19)

Pray

Arrive early (p. 88)

Prayer-walk and prepare the meeting space (p. 88)

Greet members and guests (p. 90)

(See Appendix 2 for more)

APPENDIX 2

SECOND ENCOUNTER OUTLINE

Assumes 60 minutes. Adjust if less time is available.

PRE-MOMENTS (15-30 MINUTES PRIOR)
Meet God in your daily quiet time (p. 19)
Pray
Arrive early (p. 88)
Prayer-walk and prepare the meeting space (p. 88)
Greet members and guests (p. 90)
Fellowship (p. 90)

EARLY MOMENTS (20 MINUTES)
Start on time (p. 91)
Welcome and announcements (p. 92)
Prayer in care groups (p. 93)
Create interest (p. 93)
Review (p. 98)
Preview (p. 99)

MIDDLE MOMENTS (25 MINUTES)
Begin with expectancy and good attitudes (p. 84)
Use the Bible: Scripture reading and examination (pp. 30, 105)
Set Scripture into context (p. 106)

Use good teaching methods to incorporate learning styles (p. 48)
Make assignments to smaller groups (p. 107)
Call for reports of groups (p. 108)
Recognize the relevance of the truth for the original audience
     (p. 151)
Allow the Holy Spirit to work (p. 125)

CLOSING MOMENTS (15 MINUTES)

Summarize and review (p. 150)
Apply truths (p. 151)
Invite and identify (p. 152)
Commit and pray (p. 154)
Preview/make assignments (p. 155)
Thank guests (p. 156)
Close in prayer (p. 156)
End on time (p. 156)

APPENDIX 3

LEARNING STYLE PREFERENCES

Check phrases that best describe the way you enjoy learning. Total the check marks.

Verbal	Visual
_____ Enjoy listening to stories	_____ Enjoy viewing artwork
_____ Like to talk	_____ Like watching TV & videos
_____ Enjoy discussions	_____ Can read maps well
_____ Like listening to debates	_____ Like taking pictures
_____ Enjoy word games	_____ Enjoy drawing
_____ Like writing and reading	_____ Easily distracted by movement
_____ Enjoy listening to music	_____ Like to see demonstrations
_____ **Total Checked**	_____ **Total Checked**
Active	**Rational**
_____ Enjoy drama and acting	_____ Like to solve puzzles
_____ Like to walk and hike	_____ Enjoy numbers and math
_____ Want to touch/feel things	_____ Good at problem solving
_____ Enjoy physical activities	_____ Prefer to work from a list
_____ Good at sports/athletics	_____ Like to go by the rules
_____ Good hand-eye coordination	_____ Can calculate in your head
_____ Cannot sit still for very long	_____ Asks a lot of questions
_____ **Total Checked**	_____ **Total Checked**

APPENDIX 4

BIBLE STUDY JOURNAL QUESTIONS

Write your responses as you go through each of the steps.

Date: _____ Passage: _____

Bible Study: *read, listen, examine*
Original context: What did God say in this verse/passage to the original hearers?

My context: And what is He saying to me?

Prayer: *praise, agree/confess, request*
What is my response to what God said in Bible study?

Commitment: *agree, commit to change*
Am I willing to do what He wants me to do? Explain.

What does He want me to do?

Obedience: *review progress/responses over the next few days*
What did I do with what God said?

APPENDIX 5

BIBLE STUDY MINISTRY COACH

Supporting the Second Encounter

This job description is focused largely on groups that meet at the church on Sunday. Adapt the duties to your context. A Bible study ministry coach's leadership and expectations can have a dramatic impact on Bible study groups. Without his or her leadership, facilities may not be ready, first impressions may be poor, and second encounters may suffer. With appropriate attention to details, many groups can avoid distractions and have great encounters with God in His Word.

Some coaches may find the following list overwhelming, but most will want to make the most difference possible. These suggestions usually only require a little time per task each week, and coaches can train and mobilize others to do some of the tasks. Some will be done monthly, and most will be carried out on the main days your groups meet with follow-up between meeting days.

The coach will want to begin slowly by adding a task each month to his or her routine. Each month he or she will want to delegate a task to another leader (such as overseeing the greeters or facility preparation). The coach should never stop praying, even though he or she can enlist others to pray.

Make the most out of the opportunity that God has given by carrying out these tasks:

30+ MINUTES BEFORE BIBLE STUDY GROUPS START:

- Pray. Spend time with God before arriving at church.

- Encourage group leaders to enlist apprentices who teach once a month and when the group leader is sick or away.

- Arrive early. Thirty minutes is usually adequate unless special meetings or plans are to occur.

- Prayer-walk the facility. Pray over meeting spaces, leadership, members, and guests who will soon occupy them.

- Ensure that the facility is clean, straight, comfortable, and ready before people arrive. Turn on room lights.

- Work with Bible study ministry secretary to ensure that group rolls are in meeting spaces.

15 MINUTES BEFORE BIBLE STUDY BEGINS:

- Greet, listen to, and help teachers. Ensure that teachers arrive on time and have the needed resources.

- Check that greeters are in place and make sure they have enough group directories and registration materials.

- Work with the Bible study ministry secretary each

week to ensure that groups have enough literature and printed announcements for members and guests.

- Address problems as needed.

AT TIME FOR BIBLE STUDY GROUPS TO START:

- Hold teachers accountable to start and end on time.

- Recognize teachers and groups doing something positive or good. Affirm them in the group and/or worship.

- Observe what is happening in every group. Between group meeting days, address positives and needs for improvement during individual coaching sessions with group leaders and begin discussion with them in advance of needing to start new groups.

- Ask the Bible study ministry secretary to report changes in groups, age divisions, and total Bible study ministry attendance and enrollment. Report that information to the pastor weekly.

ONCE PER MONTH:

- Walk the church facilities and observe available space and anticipated needs. Inform appropriate church leaders in advance of anticipated space problems.

- Walk the church parking lot and count the cars. Inform church leaders in advance of anticipated parking problems due to attendance growth.

- Enlist substitute teachers when teachers or their substitutes are regularly missing without notice.

TIME FOR WORSHIP:

- Promote Bible study groups. Announce attendance and invite worship attenders to be in a group next week.

- Make announcements about upcoming Bible study ministry plans.

- Recognize one or more groups and ask someone to share a two-minute Bible study group testimony each month.

Decide where to start this month. Focus on the one thing that will have the most impact. Add a new task to your routine each week or month. Give others responsibility for some of the tasks as soon as possible. Avoid going through the motions as Bible study ministry director. Work with teachers to enable revolutionary second encounters.

MEET THE AUTHOR

Darryl H. Wilson graduated from Belmont University (BA, 1982) and Southern Baptist Theological Seminary (MDiv/ CE, 1985 and EdD, 2003). He began teaching Bible study groups at age nineteen. Since 1997, he has served God and 2,400 churches as the Sunday School & Discipleship Consultant for the Kentucky Baptist Convention. These years, following fourteen years of church staff experience in Kentucky and South Carolina, added passion for the church, Sunday School, and small groups. He has authored *The Sunday School Revolutionary* blog since 2006 and serves on the Faculty and Academic Council for Rockbridge Seminary. Darryl and his wife have two sons and six grandchildren. For fun, he enjoys reading, golf, chess, and the beach.

OTHER BOOKS WITH CONTENT FROM DARRYL
Be a Catalyst: Start New Groups
Lead Your Group (PDF)
How to Sunday School Manual
Lead to Revitalize

CONNECT WITH DARRYL

BLOGS, SOCIAL MEDIA, AND VIDEOS:

Blogs (sign up for delivery by email):
www.sundayschoolrevolutionary.com
www.28nineteen.com
www.sundayschoolleader.com **(contributor)**

SOCIAL MEDIA:

https://twitter.com/DarrylWilson
https://www.facebook.com/darryl.wilson.332
https://www.linkedin.com/in/darrylwilson1

ONLINE VIDEOS:

MULTIPLY Training (password "multiply"):
http://vimeo.com/album/2774771

CARING
CARING FOR MEMBERS AND FRIENDS
The iCare Revolutionary Sunday School and Bible Study Method

In a world that is struggling under the weight of busyness and loneliness, change is much needed. It's time to refocus on relationships and care. It's time to stand up and say, "I care."

Jesus said, *"I give you a new command: Love one another. Just as I have loved you, you are also to love one another. By this everyone will know that you are my disciples, if you love one another."* If you love Him and care for others like He did, everyone will know you belong to Him.

You can lead your Bible study group to care like Jesus. When your Bible study group cares for Him and each other, His love spills beyond the walls where we gather. It touches family and friends. Every act and conversation displays His love at school, work, play, and the marketplace. A caring Bible study group is the ideal place to practice and launch that kind of love. May this book help you lead your group to demonstrate, "We care!"

Available where books are sold.